GHOST STORIES
of NORTH CAROLINA

Edrick Thay

Lone Pine Publishing International

© 2005 by Lone Pine Publishing International Inc.
First printed in 2005 10 9 8 7 6 5 4 3 2 1
Printed in Canada
All rights reserved. No part of this work covered by the copyrights hereon may be reproduced or used in any form or by any means—graphic, electronic or mechanical—without
the prior written permission of the publishers, except for reviewers, who may quote brief
passages. Any request for photocopying, recording, taping or storage on information
retrieval systems of any part of this work shall be directed in writing to the publisher.

The Publisher: Lone Pine Publishing International
Distributed by Lone Pine Publishing
1808 B Street NW, Suite 140
Auburn, WA 98001
USA

Websites: www.lonepinepublishing.com
www.ghostbooks.net

National Library of Canada Cataloguing in Publication Data

Thay, Edrick, 1977-
  Ghost stories of North Carolina / Edrick Thay.

  ISBN-13: 978-1-894877-73-2
  ISBN-10: 1-894877-73-X

  1. Ghosts--North Carolina. 2. Tales--North Carolina. I. Title.

GR110.N8T48 2005   398.2'09757'05   C2005-904483-7

Photo Credits: Every effort has been made to accurately credit photographers. Any errors or
omissions should be directed to the publisher for changes in future editions. The photographs
and illustrations in this book are reproduced with the kind permission of the following
sources: Library of Congress (p. 4-5: HABS, NC, 60-CHAR,1-1; p. 12: HABS, NC,6-CHAR,1-
2; p. 15: HABS, NC,60-CHAR,1-4; p. 27: USZ62-79409; p. 45: HABS, NC,60-CHAR,1-21; p.
57: USZ62-101486; p. 61: John Grafton, *The Civil War*, Dover Publications; p. 92, 96: HABS,
NC,7-BATH,3-1; p. 149: HABS, NC,65-WILM,4-4; p. 159: HABS, NC,65-WILM,4-6 ; p. 162:
HABS, NC,65-WILM,4-5; p. 175: HABS, NC,46-MURF,6-1; p. 196, 212: USF34-052696-D);
Istock (p. 70: Roger Pilkington; p. 80: K. Bain; p. 65, 86: Iwona Adamus; p. 111: Sharon
Dominick; p. 237: Jerry Whaley); North Wind Picture Archives (p. 134); Nick Reiter (p. 198);
Reed Mine Historic Site (p. 144, 146).

The stories, folklore and legends in this book are based on the author's collection of
sources including individuals whose experiences have led them to believe they have
encountered phenomena of some kind or another. They are meant to entertain, and neither the publisher nor the author claims these stories represent fact.

PC: P6

To My My, Cinder Block, Wench and Jessie.

Contents

Chapter 4: Public Phantoms

Chapter 5: Tragedies and Mysteries

Acknowledgments

As ever, there are many individuals to whom I'm indebted for their invaluable help, direct or indirect, in the research and writing of this book. Without their assistance, this volume would certainly not exist.

For allowing me the continued opportunity to write, I would like to thank Ghost House Books and especially Gary Whyte, Nancy Foulds and Shane Kennedy.

For helping trim my verbiage and confer upon my words a sense of narrative coherence, I must extend my gratitude to Wendy Pirk and Rachelle Delaney.

For transforming a visually plain and dull document into the glorious and magnificent book you hold now in your hands, I offer not just my appreciation, but also my continued awe to Ghost House's Production Department and Trina Koscielnuk for the work that you do.

For providing me with assistance in the sometimes agonizing search for ghost stories, I thank the paranormal investigators of North Carolina. I must reserve special thanks for Jim Hall, David Gurney and all at Haunted North Carolina Paranormal Investigators and Researchers. Your generosity and openness were wonderful and beyond my capacity to quantify. This book would simply not have existed without your help and your own special dedication to your craft.

For blazing ghost writing trails throughout the Carolinas, I would like to acknowledge and thank writers Terrance Zepke and Nancy Roberts, whose volumes will always remain the definitive sources for ghost stories.

For allowing me to ask countless questions and to intrude upon their lives, I must thank all those who offered to share their true accounts with me. I hope that you know who you are.

For moral support and laughter, I extend, as ever, my gratitude to writer-in-arms Dan Asfar. For friendship and smiles, I thank my family and friends. For buying this book, thank you readers.

Finally, for offering support that truly transcends all familial obligations, I owe my brother, Eldwin Thay, a debt that I'm sure I'll never ever be able to repay fully. His is a generosity without bounds and without his kindness, I would have suffered far more than I already have.

Introduction

I first fell in love with the state of North Carolina as a high school freshman when a bunch of friends and I went to the local multiplex to catch a little film called *The Last of the Mohicans*, which proved itself to be not just a wonderful piece of entertainment, but also a true showcase for the majestic splendors of the state's Blue Mountains. I'm certain many a Tar Heel is sick to death of the film and its association with the state, but rest assured, my affection for North Carolina is true. Bred in the Rockies, I thought myself immune to the allure of the Appalachians, but I was utterly wrong. When I decided to pursue an education in journalism, I was terribly pleased to learn that the University of North Carolina at Chapel Hill offered one of the top programs in the country. I applied but to my great chagrin was ultimately rejected, and I went off to the Midwest instead to become a Hoosier with no regrets. Of course, I'd have just as gladly become a Tar Heel.

North Carolina, quite simply, is a fascinating place. From the pristine shores of the Outer Banks to the majestic ridges and crags of the Blue Mountains, it is a land of contrasts. So it is with its history. As I delved into its past, its allure proved all the more magnetic. Roanoke Island was home to the New World's first English colony. North Carolina was arguably the first state to declare independence from imperial mother Great Britain in 1775, though following the American Revolution, it would be the 12th state to join the Union. Kitty Hawk, North Carolina, is the birthplace of mechanized flight. Reed Gold Mine was the site of the country's first great gold rush. The Raleigh-Durham area is consistently ranked among the best places to live in the United States. Two American presidents, Andrew Johnson and James Polk, were born in the state, and other illustrious North Carolinians include, to name a few, journalist David Brinkley, legendary sportscaster Howard Cosell, screen siren Ava Gardner, actor Andy Griffith, celebrated author Thomas Wolfe, legendary jazz pianist Thelonious Monk and, of course, tobacco industrialist James B. Duke. In the land where tobacco was king, North Carolina, like the rest of the agrarian states of the South, provided much of the wealth without which colonial America might very well have ceased to be. Of course, North Carolina also has its dark past, notably the slavery upon which its tobacco economy thrived. On May 20, 1861, the state seceded from the Union and plunged itself into the maelstrom of the Civil War. During that bloody conflict, nearly 40,000 North Carolinians died defending the Confederacy. The state was finally restored to the Union on July 4, 1868.

North Carolina's history looms large throughout the state. Historic landmarks such as Thalian Hall in Wilmington and Harper House at Bentonville, and homes such as the Brunswick Inn in Southport and the notorious Hammock House in Beaufort, abound. Through their preservation and restoration the past breathes again. Of course, in some places, the past never needed to be resuscitated, never having left. North Carolina is home to a great number of ghosts and legends that have drawn national attention and that, like the state itself, provide a rich tapestry testifying to the human experience. Take, for example, the great fascination with which President James Garfield sought out the Maco Light, a spectral light that appears when the spirit of brakeman Joe Baldwin returns to find his severed head. And then there is the fascinating story of the Devil's Tramping Ground, a place where it is reported (to the great derision of some and wonder of others) that the Prince of Darkness himself roams. We cannot forget the Brown Mountain Lights, a phenomenon witnessed for centuries, provoking the curiosity of the Native people who first populated the region, then that of the colonials, and now, the 21st century's allegedly science-savvy minds.

The ghosts speak of tragedies great and small. At Bentonville and Fort Fisher, sites of two of the bloodiest battles ever fought on North Carolina soil, Civil War specters rise from the mists to walk the earth again. Just outside of Jamestown, the mournful Lydia, who lost her life so many years ago in a car crash, still waits upon the side of the road on rainy nights, trying desperately to return home.

Then there are the specters who speak to the common wonders of our shared human existences. These ghosts cry out with the pain of unrequited love and lost love. The Brown Lady of Chowan College died of a broken heart when her great love never returned from the Civil War. Wealth the likes of which had never been seen couldn't keep Edith Stuyvesant Vanderbilt immune to a broken heart, and even now she continues to sit ensconced within the palatial splendor of America's largest home at Biltmore Estate.

These are but a few examples of the hundreds of stories comprising North Carolina's haunted folklore. All of them are included in this collection, as well as others many Tar Heels will surely find familiar and a few that may prove to be a pleasant surprise. For those versed in North Carolina's haunted past, I hope these retellings of popular tales will provide at least some of the joy you experienced when you first heard them. For others, I hope these stories will provide you a portrait, albeit fleeting and incomplete at best, of North Carolina's spectral side. At the very least, I hope they prove entertaining and that they may help, as they did for me, to deepen whatever affection you may hold for the Tar Heel State.

1
Haunted Houses

White Oaks

White Oaks is perhaps the most splendid of the colonial mansions that once lined the streets of Myers Park in Charlotte, North Carolina. The home once spanned 15 immaculately groomed acres, with splendid fountains to catch the eye, and boasted 52 rooms and two enormous wings. In addition to its Old World charms and opulence, White Oaks is the only house that tobacco king and noted philanthropist James Buchanan Duke ever owned in the state with which he's synonymous, and it's also quite possibly the finest home a ghost ever did haunt. In life, the ghost had been Jon Avery; in death, he's better known as a spectral symbol of undiminished love, unrequited though it may have been. He cuts quite the tragic figure and though he may only be a footnote in North Carolina history when compared to James Buchanan Duke, his story breathes life back into White Oaks.

Not much is known about Jon Avery save for the last years of his life. He and his family had moved into White Oaks where he and his wife hoped to settle into a restive retirement. It wasn't meant to be. His wife descended, slowly and agonizingly, into madness until she bore only a physical resemblance to the woman he had married. Reluctantly, he accepted his physician's recommendation and had his wife committed to a hospital. He visited often, though as she began to stare ever more blankly at the wall behind him, his resolve waned.

About this time, a reporter for a local paper arrived at White Oaks to write about the mansion's glorious history.

As she walked the brick terrace lined with lush gardens of dogwoods and azaleas, and ran her hand beneath the cool flowing waters of the marble fountains, the reporter was entranced. Then she met Jon Avery, and she was captivated. She stammered her way through the interview, not quite able to get out the questions she meant to ask. Avery was similarly struck and he found himself, to his delighted surprise, asking the reporter out to dinner. Though dimly aware of his wife's condition, she gladly accepted.

Their romance blossomed and not even the dogwood blooms could match its brilliance. But then reality reared its ugly head. She heard the whispers and saw the pointed stares of the society types who clucked disapprovingly as she walked the streets. "There she goes," they said. "Poor Mrs. Avery!" Their's was a scandalous relationship and she grudgingly accepted that high society would never brook a union. Avery's good name would forever be tarnished and hers, once quietly and pleasantly ignored, would be bandied about in derision and scorn. There was no future here—not a desirable one anyway. The reporter made the painful decision to end the relationship. Avery, though heartbroken, realized the truth of what she spoke. Before they parted, he asked for one last favor: for her to meet him a year hence, regardless of circumstance, whether they be dead or alive, at 10 minutes to midnight in the circular garden near the fountains and brick terrace. She could not deny him and promised to be there.

A year later, Avery walked hopefully out onto his terrace to wait for the reporter. At 10 minutes to midnight, she appeared, stunning as ever even in the pale blue glow of moonlight. Much had changed, yet at the same time, much had remained the same. She was betrothed to another but as

White Oaks is perhaps the most splendid mansion in Myers Park.

she lingered with Avery beneath the gently rustling leaves of the majestic trees that lined the garden, something of what they had lost was, like a precious gift, returned to them. They departed after again promising to meet at 10 to midnight, a year later.

The reporter returned as she promised but she did not come alone; she came with a roommate. Some say she no longer truly loved Avery, but the more romantically inclined argue that the roommate was there only to guarantee that her heart remain true to her fiancé. Ten to midnight came and went with no sign of Avery. The reporter continued to wait and then, like a whisper, she heard his steps soft upon the wind, light and almost ethereal. She turned and there he was, walking across the terrace. He seemed fragile and haggard, as if he had traveled far to see her. As he approached, she opened her arms wide to embrace him but watched, stunned, as his figure passed right through her. Although he spoke no words, she heard his voice clearly in her head uttering, "Dead or alive."

Only later did the reporter learn that Jon Avery had died weeks earlier. Upon hearing his last words, she wept. Laying frail on his deathbed, Avery had used his last breath to whisper, "Dead or alive? Will I make it?" Even as death drew ever closer and the sun prepared to set on his life, Avery thought not of his mortality but of the reporter who had captured his heart and to whom he had made a promise. As his body lay resting in a cemetery, his spirit carried on, determined to reach out just one last time.

The reporter returned the following year to the mansion. He had shown such devotion, even during the dimming of his own life that she expected no less of herself. At 10 to midnight, she heard Avery's footsteps. He passed through her body once again, whispering "Goodbye." The reporter never returned to White Oaks. It was far too much for her broken heart to bear. Avery's ghost was never seen again. It's comforting to think that he's found peace in the afterlife, his spirit held aloft upon the wings of unfettered and transcendental love.

George

Given that picturesque Wilmington, North Carolina is one of
the state's oldest cities, it stands to reason that it should boast
an eclectic collection of spirits and haunted houses. Among
the most famous is George, permanent resident of Price
House, which has been called Price-Gause House, 514 Market
Street. George achieved something of celebrity status in 1967
when his spirit, a misty shapeless form, was caught, in a
photograph, descending a staircase. Though the spirit's been
baptized George, his true identity remains a mystery. He
might even be a she. All anyone knows for sure is that whoever the ghost is, he or she is certainly fond of three things:
pranks, pipes and yams.

Price House, according to Wilmington folklore, rests, like
many of the surrounding homes, on the former hanging
grounds of 19th-century Wilmington, known once upon a
time as Gallows Hill. Countless criminals were sent to their
early graves on the knoll, and then were allegedly buried
nearby. Some say one of them never really left. When the city
began to creep across its original boundaries and land was
needed to accommodate the influx of citizens, the gallows
were torn down and houses were erected; some were over the
burial grounds. Built in 1855 or 1860 (no one seems to know
for sure), Price House, named for the man who had it built,
was constructed in the Italianate style with red brick. It's a
quaint little place with deep blue shutters framing its windows and an elegant covered porch of white columns. It's
been haunted from the start.

Its first residents, Lieutenant Colonel William Jones Price and his family, hadn't even been in the place for a week before eerie things began happening. From upstairs, in the bedrooms and the attic, the Prices heard loud thumps and heavy footfalls. As a trained professional soldier, Lieutenant Colonel Price didn't scare easy. Grabbing his rifle and fixing its bayonet, Price ascended the staircase with grim determination and explored the upper floors room by room. But he found nothing unusual. Everything was in order, and while he found a rat here and there, surely they couldn't have been responsible for the heavy thumps and footsteps he'd heard. Now, Price was genuinely frightened.

The sounds continued, waking the family during the night and assailing them throughout the day. Then the ghost grew bolder. It seemed that overnight, the Price family had developed a habit of misplacing everything. They'd put something down on a table only to discover it, days later, hidden somewhere else. Foodstuffs went missing from their larder. Price initially accused his children of playing a prank, but then realized it couldn't have been them. They were too short to have reached the highest shelves of the pantry. And they certainly couldn't have been behind the tapping that seemed to come from behind the walls.

Price quickly came to the conclusion that they were dealing with a spirit. It comforted him to know that this one, though mischievous, seemed to mean no harm. In time, as they became more familiar and comfortable with the ghost's routine, they came to accept the spirit as part of the family, referring to it often as "our ghost." The Prices eventually moved from the house with just one regret. They wished that they could have discerned more about their lively houseguest.

The Gauses moved into 514 Market Street quite aware of the house's past. While living with the ghost, they always felt as if they were the guests and the ghost was the host. The family would wake in the morning and find the kitchen a mess—dirty forks and knives and stained napkins littered the table. The sweet aroma of what could only be sweet potatoes baking in an oven often lingered in the air. The Gause children found the spirit more than a little frustrating. They'd have to make their beds at least twice a day for the ghost was quite fond of pulling up sheets and tossing pillows. When it had had enough, it would retire to its favorite rocking chair where, invisible, it would light up a smoke, filling the room with the scent of pipe tobacco, and rock back and forth in the chair.

The house later became so famous (or infamous) that in 1967, a Wilmington newspaper decided to investigate the phenomenon. Its editor sent a reporter and photographer to the home. For two days, the two waited for something amazing to happen. They walked around the house, examining rooms and hoping to find something that might corroborate all the fantastic stories they'd heard. But nothing happened. The reporter and photographer had all but left when they heard what sounded like the hurried, heavy footsteps of someone (or something) running across the upstairs hall. Cutting quick, excited glances at each other, the intrepid duo clattered up the stairs but found nothing, save for a rocking chair mysteriously swaying back and forth. Aside from the mother of the family, who was downstairs working in the kitchen, the reporter and photographer were alone.

As they stood there, examining the chair and windows (just in case a breeze had blown through the room and disturbed the chair), the two newsmen felt something brush past them with what writer Terrance Zepke calls a "swishing sound." Camera at the ready, the photographer rushed into the hall and began snapping pictures. Eagerly, they returned to the newsroom to develop the shots and see what might have been captured on celluloid.

As the images came to life beneath the red lights of the darkroom, the two sighed and shook their heads. There was nothing unusual in the first one. Or the second. But as the third materialized, they felt their breath catch in their throats. They weren't exactly sure what they were looking at, but they were certain that, at the very least, it had to be a ghost. The thing had no discernible figure or shape, but rather appeared as a sort of milky mist.

For years, Wilmington's Chamber of Commerce called the place home and its employees found the place as strange as the Prices and the Gauses had. Lights and faucets turned on and off, and typewriters mysteriously malfunctioned. They attributed all of these unexplained disturbances to George, who seemed undeniably fascinated with all the technological marvels and conveniences of the 20th century. But none outstripped the spirit's love for some good ol'-fashioned down-home cooking and a good smoke. Employees have recalled that the Chamber of Commerce often smelled like pipe smoke and yams.

The Chamber of Commerce departed a few years ago, making way for the architectural firm BMS Architects, which renovated the place. Although in many cases, renovations tend to provoke spirits who are resistant to change, George has happily adapted. He's quite fond of opening the front door and watching with glee as an architect peers out the entrance only to find an empty porch. His footsteps, which were once mostly heard only at night, ring throughout the place all day long. He's become so commonplace that no one bats an eye. And, as ever, George loves his tobacco and a warm serving of oven-browned sweet potatoes.

Mordecai Manor

Had it not been for Wake County plantation owner Joel Lane, the North Carolina capital of Raleigh might be a very different place. In the late 18th century, Lane's plantation was one of the largest in Wake County. It produced everything from vegetables to medicinal herbs. The centerpiece of it all was a glorious mansion that Lane had constructed for his son, Henry, in 1785. It was the social hub from which radiated the spokes of the local communities. When city planners arrived to lay out a grid for the city of Raleigh, they first considered land that belonged to Colonel John Hinton across the Neuse River. Lane, never one to miss an opportunity to increase his wealth, meant to thwart Hinton. On the eve of the committee's vote, Lane invited high-ranking officials to his home for food and drink. Swayed by Lane's generous gesture, the committee chose in favor of Lane. For £1378, the committee purchased 1000 acres of Lane's plantation, and Raleigh was born.

When Joel Lane passed away, his holdings passed to son Henry and his family. Among Henry's children was a daughter named Margaret. She married Moses Mordecai, a prominent Raleigh lawyer and judge, and bore him three children. Margaret fell ill and passed away when she was still very young. Ownership of her family home passed to Mordecai.

Mordecai, ever loyal to the Lane family, quickly remarried, choosing as his wife Margaret's sister, Ann. Together they had one more child before Mordecai himself succumbed to an illness in 1824. His will stipulated that his lavish mansion be expanded further. Two years later, the expansion was complete. Even though the house had lost its patriarch, the Lane plantation survived and even prospered. When they were grown up, the Mordecai children assumed positions of prominence within Raleigh's social elite, and their plantation served as the Mordecai family seat for five consecutive generations. The plantation was so large that even after the Civil War had ravaged its prominence and prosperity, three separate neighborhoods were created out of land from the plantation. But while one of the neighborhoods bears Mordecai's name today, Margaret Lane means to ensure that the contributions of her family and its place in Raleigh's history are not forgotten.

In 1967, the city of Raleigh bought the plantation home, along with its furnishings, to preserve and honor the Mordecai legacy. The home was restored to its previous splendor, as were a number of other structures around the plantation, including a stone house, a kitchen and a garden. The city also decided to move other historical structures from around Raleigh to the plantation site, including a post office dating from 1847, a law office from 1810 and a church from 1840. Thus the Mordecai Historical Park began—a living museum in more ways than one.

The park's centerpiece and most popular attraction is without question the Mordecai Manor, a two-story mansion open to the visiting public. To enhance the authentic experience, the house has been decorated with 18th- and 19th-century furnishings. A dedicated group of guides and cleaning staff care for the home, sweeping out and wiping up the day's dust each night.

One humid afternoon, a housekeeper was hard at work in the dining room. She worked carefully and deliberately, in no hurry. The place was closed to the public at the time and she enjoyed the peace and the quiet. With the dining room clean, she moved into the hallway to clean the woodwork framing the dining room entrance.

As she worked, something caught her attention. A manor guide walked out of the library. Normally, the housekeeper wouldn't have thought twice about it, but she'd thought all the guides had already gone home for the day. Wasn't she the only staff member in the house? Then there was the guide's clothing. She was dressed…well, she was dressed oddly, more than a little out of step with the fashions of the day. The guide was wearing a long black pleated skirt, a white blouse and a black tie. But still, there was something reassuring and familiar about the woman and the housekeeper just assumed that the guide had stayed behind to catch up on some work.

The guide drew near the housekeeper. The housekeeper, never one to be rude, turned from the woodwork and as she wiped the sweat from her brow, waved and said hello to the woman. But the guide continued walking. She didn't even break her stride and completely ignored the housekeeper. There was a confidence and an assurance to the guide's walk—an imperial bearing that suggested she was above the lowly housekeeper. Her curiosity and anger piqued, the housekeeper watched as the guide continued into the parlor. The housekeeper followed, unwilling to let the slight go ignored. But when she entered the parlor, there was no one there. The room was empty and the housekeeper was as alone as she had originally suspected herself to be.

The housekeeper looked from one end of the room to the other. Except for the gentle rustling of the curtains swaying in the afternoon breeze, everything was still and quiet. She scratched her head. Where could the guide have gone? She was standing in the room's only entrance—and therefore its only exit—and she was certain that no one had passed her. Then her gaze happened to fall upon a large portrait from which Margaret Lane stared out upon the room. With a gasp, the housekeeper realized why the guide had seemed so familiar. The woman she had seen was no employee of Mordecai Manor. She had caught a glimpse of nothing less than the spirit of Margaret Lane Mordecai, first wife of Moses Mordecai and the first lady of Mordecai Manor.

Margaret Lane Mordecai may not have been the first woman to live in the landmark, but she was the first to live in the home under its current name. In life, her authority was complete; it has been said that Mrs. Mordecai was stern but never harsh, and that her great affection for her husband and children was rivaled only by that for her home. It's no surprise that the woman has returned. She spent the happiest years of her life at Mordecai Manor. She has returned in death, seemingly determined to make sure that Mordecai Manor staff hold up to the same high standards she expected of her own staff in life.

Biltmore Estate

The Gilded Age of the late 19th century was an era of explosive and tremendous social upheaval. Society, for the first time, was beginning to reap the rewards of the mass-produced abundance of modern industrialization. Those people fortunate enough to stake a claim achieved unprecedented wealth and celebrated their unimaginable fortunes in an orgy of largesse, indulgence and overt affluence. It was the age of Rockefeller, Carnegie, Astor, Morgan and Vanderbilt, the families who dominated society and culture like the titans of industry that they were and who lived by a credo best articulated by Mark Twain. "What is the chief end of man?" Twain once wrote. "To get rich. In what way? Dishonestly if we can; honestly if we must." These families ruled from high; they threw lavish parties and erected mansions along New York City's Fifth Avenue while the huddled masses shivered and toiled. As the exclusive and select ranks of the rich luxuriated in their wealth, the majority of America suffered through poverty. In 1890, 11 million of America's 12 million families earned less than $1200 a year; the average income for the poorest group was $380, well below the poverty line. So were born the tenements and slums, breeding grounds of the great national discontent that heralded the arrival of the Progressive Era of the early 20th century and Franklin Roosevelt's New Deal. Such was the legacy of the Gilded Age.

The Gilded Age today is suffused with the soft and forgiving glow of romanticism, its excesses tempered with nostalgia. Despite its rotten core, at its best the Gilded Age represents and embodies the great optimism of the American Dream; it

George Washington Vanderbilt II's Biltmore Estate—a place so magnificent that its builder and his wife never left.

was a world in which anything was possible, in which industry and ingenuity promised a utopic civilization where anyone could realize the full extent of his potential. It's a vision represented in the grand homes and estates the great families of the Gilded Age left behind. Rosecliff, Breakers, Marble House, The Elms: these are the windows to the past, though none are more clear and unblemished than George Washington Vanderbilt II's Biltmore Estate in the shadows of the Blue Mountains—a place so magnificent, awesome and fantastic that its builder and wife never left.

The history of the Vanderbilts is the stuff of Horatio Alger. From humble farming origins, the Vanderbilt family rose to become the wealthiest of all the Gilded Age families with a staggering fortune unimaginable today.

Jan Aertsen Van der Bilt emigrated from Holland to the New World in 1650, and he and his descendants turned to farming to earn a modest lifestyle, working the lands of Staten Island, New York. It all changed with the arrival of The Commodore, Cornelius Vanderbilt. In an oft-told and apocryphal account, Cornelius borrowed $100 from his mother to launch a ferry service in New York. Within a few short years, he had turned his one small steamboat into a fleet of 100, ferrying passengers across the globe, from Central America to Europe. Not content with dominating the ocean, Cornelius turned his attention to the fledgling railroad business and earned yet another fortune. The Commodore had multiplied his mother's $100 a million-fold to become the wealthiest industrialist in the United States.

The Commodore died in 1877 and left most of his $100 million to the eldest of his 13 children, William Henry, who was intelligent, industrious and blessed with an understanding of commerce (he was not above bribing railroad officials investigating his preferential treatment of passengers). William Henry, in nine short years, doubled his family's wealth to become the richest man ever in American history. When he died in 1885, his substantial wealth was dispersed amongst his eight children, though the bulk of it went to his four sons. Among them was the youngest child, George Washington Vanderbilt II.

George was only 13 when his father passed away. He was the only child still living at the family mansion on the stretch of Fifth Avenue known simply as Millionaire's Row. George and his mother were understandably close and her influence upon the youngest Vanderbilt was clear. The young boy was quiet and intellectual, possessing little interest in either high society or the family business. He preferred literature, art and horticulture, and whereas his father and grandfather had both been blessed with a strong Protestant work ethic, he was noticeably idle. He certainly appreciated his father's wealth, spending the large inheritance on a lifestyle of excess. Like many of his ilk, George fancied himself the heir of a great western tradition born in the glories of the Greek and Roman Empires and the Renaissance. As such, he spent much of his time traveling the world, collecting art and books and partaking in the Grand Tour in favor with the moneyed upper class. He frequented Paris and roamed as far as Asia. But as exotic as the European and Asian continents were, George found something particularly attractive and restful in the Blue Mountains of North Carolina.

In 1888, construction began on the Biltmore Estate. He had chosen the name Biltmore to honor Bildt, the Dutch region from which his forebears hailed, and then combined it with the old English word *more*, meaning "upland rolling hills" to reflect its pastoral surroundings. Designed by famed architect Richard Morris Hunt, Biltmore was modeled after three 16th-century French chateaux in the famed Loire Valley. The house, or to be more accurate, palace, had 4 acres of living space alone (the equivalent of 88 modern average-sized homes), 250 rooms, 34 bedrooms, 43 bathrooms, 65 fireplaces and more than 60 staff rooms. There was a swimming pool that required 70,000 gallons of water to fill and a library that housed his 23,000 volumes. The building was the jewel of a 125,000-acre estate, designed and laid out by Central Park designer Frederick Law Olmsted. Construction took six years; the work site had its own brick factory that produced more than 32,000 bricks a day, a woodworking shop and three-mile railroad spur for the transportation of materials. Biltmore Estate was the very embodiment of the technological marvels of the Gilded Age. It boasted central heating, hot and cold running water, walk-in coolers and electrical lighting. It was, and is, the largest home in the United States. On Christmas Eve, 1895, George welcomed his family to the completed Biltmore Estate.

With his castle completed, George devoted his energies to his passions: art, literature and horticulture. His art collection boasted works from Renoir and Whistler, and he oversaw experiments in scientific farming, animal bloodline breeding and silviculture. The estate became a community all its own, with dozens of families working and farming the land. In the fall, harvest fairs were held with prizes awarded to the best fresh fruits and vegetables, needlework and flower arrangements.

In 1898, while in Paris, George married Edith Stuyvesant Dresser and together they returned to Biltmore, where their only child, Cornelia Stuyvesant Vanderbilt, was born. They were the only Vanderbilts to ever call Biltmore home. George's profligate lifestyle, coupled with the enormous costs required to maintain the estate and countless bad investments, had all but depleted his once-substantial fortune. He died in Washington in 1914 after undergoing an emergency appendectomy. Edith, in the face of rising costs, sold much of the 125,000 acres upon which Biltmore rested to the United States Forest Service, which, in turn, created the Pisgah National Forest.

In 1930, with the nearby city of Asheville crippled like the rest of the country by the Great Depression, Cornelia and her husband, John Amherst Cecil, opened the Biltmore to the public. Asheville city officials had hoped that the resulting tourism would bolster its faltering economy. In just a few short years, the dream of Biltmore, a privileged oasis that George had built for the exclusive use of his family and friends, had passed into history along with the Gilded Age. Its hold on the public's imagination, however, has never wavered.

Since it opened to the public, the Biltmore has been a popular attraction. A Vanderbilt still claims ownership: George's grandson, William Cecil. It draws 900,000 visitors a year to its 8000 acres, its magnificent rose and azalea gardens (containing over 2300 roses and around 1000 azaleas), its winery and of course, the home itself. Among its more celebrated guests are Jacqueline Kennedy Onassis, Prince Charles, U.S. presidents William McKinley, Theodore Roosevelt and Jimmy Carter, and modern American royalty in the form of Robert Redford, Tom Hanks and Bill Gates. Its popularity has much to do with the loving attention to detail the Biltmore's 1500-strong staff bring to its maintenance and care. At Biltmore Estate, the Gilded Age is still very much alive…in more ways than one.

When George Washington Vanderbilt II died unexpectedly, his wife Edith was left a heartbroken widow. According to local folklore, she took to sitting by the library's marble fireplace well into the night. Often, she could be heard talking softly and when her staff inquired as to whom she might be speaking, she would answer simply, "George." It's said that late at night, even now, Edith still speaks to her late husband.

Her whispers have startled more than one Biltmore Estate
employee. George himself can be found frequenting his
favorite rooms, the Billiard Room and a second-floor sitting
room. When the night is dark and the rain is falling, George
might just appear to indulge a favorite pastime of his: reading one of his many volumes in his favorite chair.

Downstairs, parties thought to be long over come to life
once again by the swimming pool where the splashing of
water and cries of laughter echo throughout the basement.
It's all in pitiful contrast to the mournful lady in black who is
the most visible and witnessed of the Biltmore Estate's resident spirits. Though no one knows what her origins may be,
her spirit is so mournful and dreadful that she has moved her
witnesses to tears. Surely hers must be a tragic tale; perhaps
she drowned long ago in an accident long forgotten.

In one of the more lively and startling accounts to come
out of the Biltmore Estate, Annie Vogel (a pseudonym)
recalls the time she went to visit the home. "I remember
thinking to myself, 'How could any place be so luxurious?'"
Annie writes. "And then I went to walk in the gardens. It just
took my breath away." It was there that Annie remembers
being startled out of her awe-stricken state. Out of the corner
of her eye, she spied someone she assumed to be a maid or
perhaps a re-enactor, "the better to recreate life at Biltmore."
The woman held a tray of champagne glasses in one hand
and held a glass out toward Annie, as if offering a drink.
Annie reached out to accept it but then, "she just up and
vanished." Annie spent the rest of the afternoon wandering
around the place in a sort of daze. "I was just blown away,"
she finishes with a hearty laugh. "But, I guess for a moment,
maybe she thought I was a Vanderbilt."

To be a Vanderbilt…the thought must surely pass through the mind of every individual who visits Biltmore Estate. George Washington Vanderbilt II built America's castle and what a castle it is: a living symbol of a bygone era, and a dream that existed for the briefest of moments to inspire and to define a nation only to collapse under the weight of its own excess.

The Haunted Farmhouse

Jim Hall has always had an interest in ghosts. Ever since he was a high school student in the mid-1980s, he "would go to [potentially haunted] places and hang out, just to see what happens and to find out if there was any truth to the stories I'd heard." Of course, these days, as a member of Haunted North Carolina Paranormal Investigators and Researchers, Hall's work isn't as simple as all that. He joined the organization, first founded in 1992 as Seven Paranormal Research, in 2001 and since then has conducted a different kind of research altogether.

"There is some specialized equipment we use to measure environmental factors," he says, "electromagnetic and geomagnetic fields, temperature levels, humidity. We're constantly experimenting with new ideas." Recently, Hall and other investigators began working with a spectroscope, a device capable, he hopes, of measuring the energy emitted by paranormal phenomena.

"On the very few rare occasions when we see something happen in real time," he explains, "the spectroscope will be able to measure energy of a system...the wavelengths of light coming off a particular reaction. If there's no physical substance to a [ghost], then you're observing some sort of interaction with the atmosphere." It's a pragmatic and reasonable approach in a field often dismissed as pseudoscience. Hall recognizes the stigma attached to such work but accepts it and hopes that, in time, the good work that he and others of his ilk are attempting to do will offer some legitimacy.

To that end, Hall always explores the science first before offering another explanation. He's happily dismissed such long-standing and beloved haunted sites as the Devil's Tramping Ground and Lydia's Bridge as being nothing more than good stories, which, while entertaining, have little or nothing to do with ghosts. According to Hall, the evidence just isn't there. "Cold spots and hot spots," he says, addressing a phenomenon often taken as proof of a paranormal presence, "I don't really know what I feel about them. So many times, you're able to find other explanations for cold spots. There's almost no environment that we can control completely. Most of the time, we're outdoors, or in some rickety old house with drafts, windows, doors and air-conditioning vents." So, in order to lend legitimacy to the phenomenon, Haunted North Carolina has set up criteria and adopted what Hall describes as an "evidential mindset": they will only examine temperature fluctuations of greater than 10 degrees. If an investigation is done outside, they demand an even wider variance.

"This work requires a lot of patience and critical thinking. You've got to be able to handle the monotony of it," he says firmly. "You've got to separate yourself emotionally and you can't go in wanting to find something. If you do, you'll interpret anything you see as proof or evidence." What galls Hall the most is the impatience of other paranormal investigators and how their attitudes often end up stereotyping them all, undermining their own work.

"It's frustrating when people make assumptions about what we do based on what other people do," he states emphatically. "What we try to do is to do research. A lot of [paranormal] groups out there, their goal is producing evidence. They want the one picture, the one EVP that proves to the world that ghosts exist. There's never going to be that one piece of evidence to convince the world." He points to the glut of EVP recordings and photographs of orbs that can be found on pretty much all paranormal web pages, evidence that he doesn't completely dismiss, but that he does find not completely convincing. Hall and his group hope to build a database of empirical evidence, to form a set of information from which they can conduct a systemic analysis to produce tangible numbers and "turn the raw data into useful forms." Sounds an awful lot like the scientific method, doesn't it?

Hall also cautions against those paranormal investigators he calls "frauds and scams": the groups that charge money for their questionable certifications. "That's kind of sketchy right there," he points out, "and to lump us in with those people is unfair. We don't all believe the same thing. And for us, we spend a lot of our money. We're all volunteers." Indeed, most of the time Hall is a Social Studies teacher, but his true passions, of course, are the ghosts. He is decidedly not in this work for the money; in that light, Hall and the other investigators of Haunted North Carolina are really no different than the struggling musician or the starving writer, individuals with a love for a craft that only rarely offers great financial rewards. Haunted North Carolina's dedication and work has not gone unnoticed.

"Probably about 90 percent of our cases result from people who contact us," he says, careful to note (with a tired laugh) that despite what people might think, Haunted North Carolina and its investigators are not "ghostbusters." He spits the word out wearily, no doubt tired of the association. What Hall and the group try to provide, for the most part, is "peace of mind" to people unfamiliar with and frightened by the paranormal.

Once that little matter is cleared up, an assigned case manager will decide whether or not a client's case is valid or if someone just wants attention. "We probably do miss out on a lot of good cases," Hall acknowledges, "but we get two or three order investigations over a day and we just can't do them all. It adds up." The case manager then reports back either to Hall or to investigator David Gurney, who decides if the case merits a deeper investigation. If it does, interviews are conducted onsite, information is gathered and the history of the property in question is sifted through "to understand what may or may not be going on there." The final step is the actual investigation itself, during which only the case manager and either Hall or Gurney are aware of the background information. "Everyone else goes in cold," Hall says. "We don't want a bias." A team of five or six people will often spend an entire night examining a property and collecting data and evidence. They may actually return on multiple occasions in order to gather new evidence and data for the group "to ponder."

Asked to share his most memorable investigation, Hall pauses to think. "It depends on why it's memorable," he says. "An investigation can be memorable for many different things, but if you're asking about sheer activity we've experienced and witnessed, it's got to be an abandoned farmhouse we first investigated in 2002."

Despite some prodding, Hall refuses to disclose the farm's location, except to say that it may or may not be around Winston-Salem. Of course, this secrecy is understandable. One need only look at the messes and detritus cluttering popular sites like the Devil's Tramping Ground and Lydia's Bridge to know why. "We've an agreement not to reveal the location," Hall explains, "but anyone within 30 miles of it knows all about it."

Haunted North Carolina first investigated the site in 2002 and has since returned multiple times. "The history of that particular location is staggering," an audibly excited Hall says. "A lot of the time, a particular house might have a legend associated with it but you can never find anything to corroborate it. With this abandoned farm, the sheer number of deaths from suicide and foul play over the last 50 years is staggering." Hall describes reading gruesome accounts of people exploding themselves with sticks of dynamite, of the Mafia-style executions of two individuals beneath the awning of an outbuilding and of the torture and grisly murder of a prostitute. Visitors to the site often reported that their cars would mysteriously stall only to start up again when pushed past a certain point.

"When the house actually existed—it burnt down 10 years ago—the last people who lived in it," Hall says, "were a woman who was a police officer and her son who was in the academy. All of this is in the police reports." Hall pauses for a dramatic second before continuing. "The son accidentally shot his girlfriend and then shortly after killed himself." And this is only information that has been verified. Hall states that there are even more stories dating back two centuries concerning the property, and while he wishes they could be corroborated, it just hasn't been possible.

According to local legend, a family living at the farm during the early 20th century experienced a mind-boggling and jaw-dropping 15 suicides within their kin, nearly all of whom lived in or around the farmhouse. Since that time, there have been numerous hangings and drownings too. Taken all together, it seems as if there's good reason why the farmhouse is abandoned and even more reason to believe that there may very well be a curse upon the land. Hall laughs at this hypothesis. "If you believe in curses and whatnot," he says, "it might qualify."

If so, then perhaps it all started in the antebellum South when a particularly vile and ruthless man ran a plantation on the grounds. The particulars of the accounts are lost and there are a number of different legends concerning the plantation owner. Regardless, he's said to have loved torturing his slaves, unaware that one of his daughters was secretly carrying on an affair with one of them. The tryst came to an ignoble end when she became pregnant. Though she tried to hide her condition, her protruding belly proclaimed loudly for all to see what she had refused to admit. Her father flew into a rage and, according to one account, killed his entire family, then burnt down the plantation. Or he may have just had the offending slave killed, or, in the most gruesome twist of all, herded the slave and a host of others into a church, locked the door and then burnt the whole thing down. Other accounts ignore the slaves altogether and paint the plantation owner instead as a worshipper of Satan who killed his family while in the Devil's grip, then put the plantation to the torch. Whatever the story, the site certainly has an undeniably intriguing history, populated with exactly the sort of macabre details that so often are at the root of paranormal phenomenon.

On their first investigation, Hall, Gurney and their team were on the receiving end of some truly bizarre occurrences. One member was taking some baseline readings when he felt something tugging on his backpack. When watched on videotape, one can plainly see the backpack actually being pulled by unseen hands. In a large tobacco shed, EVP recordings were taken and when played back later, investigators could hear multiple plaintive voices calling, "Help us." In a corncrib, temperatures fluctuated wildly, as much as 30 degrees at times. One investigator distinctly felt someone touch her hand. The invisible touch left a red welt on her skin. When she left the corncrib, she again felt something; this time, someone's invisible hand brushed her hair.

In the remains of what was once the main house, the investigators set up audio recording equipment with the hopes of capturing EVP. When played back later, investigators were delighted to hear that they had indeed done exactly that. The first EVP recording sounds very much like the chiming of a bell, which investigators "likened to a tuning fork being struck." The second is of a "short cry followed by…distinct raps on a door or table." The third is actual speech, completely distinct and rising above the static. According to the Haunted North Carolina website, the voice says "hello," in an odd flat inflection with an odd speech pattern." It all dovetailed nicely with the video recording another member made in a shed behind the remnants of the main house at the same time.

The camera was set up and left to film undisturbed. When watched later, the camera's auto-focus feature kicked into gear even though nothing visible had appeared in its field of vision. At the same time, what sounded like a plodding footstep could be heard inside the building; the footsteps then increased in volume, as if someone or something were approaching the camera. Then, there's only silence as the camera refocused itself. Many pictures taken that night have bizarre anomalies. Hall says that within them, you can see "houses that weren't there…one had a light anomaly and in it, you can see the porch." Along a riverbank, all but four of the investigators witnessed an apparition. After initially mistaking the shadowy form for one of their own, the researchers quickly realized that they were watching a ghost. As it approached them, a mysteriously dense fog rose up behind it, dissipating only when the ghost faded into the night. The material gathered was promising to say the least, and with such an abundance of evidence, the group eagerly planned another investigation. The second visit yielded even more intriguing results.

The team arrived at the abandoned farmstead shortly after sundown and quickly set about placing their equipment around the site. This time, in order to better identify the source of the strange sounds they had heard earlier, the group set up multiple cameras and audio recorders. Two investigators were assigned the task of watching the building from the outside at all times to ensure that their samples remain unspoiled by human interaction.

When investigator Matt Sweeney (the man who had had his backpack grabbed) finished setting up a camera in the house, he walked away commenting, "I bet as soon as we walk off, one of these ghosts is going to walk up to the camera and go, 'Bong!'" They didn't know it at the time, but Sweeney's prediction was completely apt. Two minutes into the recording, investigators could hear what Hall describes as a "very faint, high-pitched voice saying, 'Bong.'" It's followed by what is undeniably the laughter of a child. The same recording captured a full eight minutes of a seemingly empty room in which a constant barrage of footsteps assaulted the audio track. Audio recordings again captured the chiming of bells, but what was most intriguing was what they had not recorded.

During the investigation, the two researchers assigned to watch the building heard what they described as a "distant metallic banging," which sounded very much like a hammer striking an anvil, echoing from across the road. They made a note of the sound, and then dismissed it as being insignificant. They assumed that it was just something off in the distance or that it was caused by two of their companions who had left to examine another area. Several minutes later, they heard the sound again, only this time it had increased in volume and sounded much closer. The two watchmen noted it once again, but this time they didn't dismiss it so casually. They heard it twice more, and the final time, they swore that it was as if the sound was right on top of them. Was it an approaching storm? Or had something happened to the other two investigators? With great urgency, they radioed the others. The rest of the team was fine but, strangely enough, had heard nothing. And the strange metallic banging was absent from any of the audio recordings. There was something oddly familiar about the experience. During the course of their preliminary research, the group had interviewed several people familiar with the site. Some spoke of a strange metallic sound that only a select few could hear.

In the most bizarre, even frightening, account, two investigators left the main house to examine another area that had yielded results on the first investigation. To get there, the two had to tramp through a field of tall, thick grass. One investigator had tucked the car keys attached to his belt into his pocket to keep them safe and prevent their tinkly jangles from interfering with sound recordings. When he returned to the main house, he realized with a start that his keys were missing. He frantically retraced his steps, plowing in vain through the tall stalks of grass. With the prospect of having to leave his automobile behind, the investigator walked to his car only to find that it was unlocked. He opened the door and to his chagrin and consternation, found his keys dangling from the ignition. Of course, he could very well have forgotten to remove the keys but several other researchers distinctly recalled seeing him remove them and even claimed they had seen him with the keys during the night-long investigation. They could only conclude that someone had removed the keys from his pocket, unhitched them from his belt and then inserted them in the ignition, all without the investigator noticing a thing. An incredible theory, to be sure, but for Haunted North Carolina Paranormal Investigators and Researchers, it's the only explanation that seems to fit. There is definitely something in the abandoned farmstead, but as yet the group has not drawn any definitive conclusions. The only certainty is that the group has in its possession a pool of evidence that will surely go a great way toward helping it build its database.

For Hall, the abandoned farmhouse, with its abundance of activity and seemingly restless spirits, must surely be akin to something like the Holy Grail. Actual interaction with a ghost is a rarity, and some investigators may go their entire careers without ever experiencing such a thing. For the most part, after the initial curiosity and fear about the paranormal has waned, the work can acquire a sort of monotony alleviated only by the intensity and dedication of an individual passion and the hope that more lies just around the corner. "If you stick with it long enough," Hall says, "something will occur on an investigation, and when it does, it's very exciting." Surely the abandoned farmhouse qualifies.

Slocumb House

First constructed at the turn of the 19th century, Slocumb House has been many things to many people over the years. For a short time in the early 19th century, it served as a United States bank. During the Civil War, the bank vault was rumored to have been converted into the entrance of a tunnel that led to the Cape Fear River. Today, it is suspected of being a haunted house, home to a restless spirit who continues to search for her murdered fiancé. For over a century, the young, beautiful woman has mournfully walked up and down the wooden staircase . She never learned of her lover's fate. Unbeknownst to her, he had been murdered in the house's basement and his body disposed of within the old bank vault some time during the Civil War.

The story has been repeated often and it first inspired noted and beloved author Nancy Roberts to begin writing ghost stories. On a visit to her mother, Roberts was treated to a story that had been told long ago to her mother by a Presbyterian minister named Dr. John Allen McLean.

It was the early 20th century and the kerosene lamps of Slocumb House in Fayetteville burned brightly, bathing partygoers in a warm, yellow glow. The house was alive with conversation and music. Fayetteville girls, their dapper suitors on their arms, crowded around the piano and sang with loud, gay voices to the tune of a romantic ballad. In the parlor, a young lawyer stood by the marble mantel carved so many years ago by Italian craftsmen. Its surface was cool to his touch and it shimmered softly in the light. Absentmindedly, he picked at a small indentation in the

For over a century, a young, beautiful woman has mournfully walked up and down the wooden staircase.

mantel's surface, allegedly left there by a bullet fired from the gun of Union General William Tecumseh Sherman.

He watched the people come and go and, despite the festive atmosphere, could think about nothing but a conundrum that had occupied his mind for days. He was a practicing lawyer, but the work left him unsatisfied. Surely there was something for which he was better suited, but if so, what could it possibly be? And was he really willing to throw away all those long and tortured years spent in law school?

He left the parlor, the noise and merriment intruding rudely upon his introspection. Just beyond the archway that opened into the parlor, the young man stood at the foot of the staircase. He placed one hand on the intricately carved banister and breathed deeply. He hadn't been standing there long before he witnessed something that would forever change his life.

As he stood with his gaze fixed on nothing in particular, a figure began descending the staircase. With a start, the man drew back, unable to breathe. The figure, a young, beautiful woman clad in a gown, was completely transparent. He could see right through her, to the stairs and landing behind her. She walked, or floated, down the steps without a sound. At the bottom, she stopped briefly before turning, slowly and sadly, to climb back up the stairs. When she reached the second-floor landing, there was a flutter and the woman was gone. The young man needed air and fled out into the spring night. He had often heard stories about the Slocumb House but until now had only accepted them as pleasing and entertaining diversions. He knew then that the stories had all been true and in that moment, he decided to abandon his plans for a law career and instead enter the ministry. The young man was none other than the Presbyterian minister Dr. John Allen McLean.

Slocumb House is a historic place. It has served as a family home, and it houses famed oil paintings painted by Elliot Dangerfield. General LaFayette walked its floors and during the Civil War, both Confederate and Union troops occupied the place. Still, for all its history and its storied past, it's the broken-hearted woman of Slocumb House that resonates most with visitors. To gaze upon her spirit descending and then ascending the staircase is to share in a human experience. It's bitter and melancholy, to be sure, but it is accessible. She is heartache personified, arousing either sympathy or empathy. Few can deny the touch of her mournful spirit.

Hammock House

As the oldest house in Beaufort, North Carolina, Hammock House has a history spanning over three centuries. It was once allegedly home to the pirate Blackbeard—in 1997, his alleged flagship, the *Queen Anne's Revenge,* was purportedly discovered just two miles from Beaufort Inlet in 20 feet of water. Hammock House also served as a residence for Union soldiers during the Civil War, an inn, a summer house and a school. Today, Hammock House, through sheer preservation and longevity, naturally occupies a prominent place in Beaufort history, a tangible connection to the colorful characters and stories of its ever-receding past. The past literally comes to life at Hammock House, the reported home to a spectral population of spooks that render the house a virtual living museum and make its history accessible.

Built at the turn of the 18th century, Hammock House sat on what were then the banks of Taylor's Creek in a fledgling community known simply as Fish Town. Straddling the inlet leading to the waters of the Atlantic Ocean, the simple white, two-story structure, flanked by great free-standing chimneys of English brick on ballast stone foundations, was visible for miles on the Atlantic and quickly became a boon to merchant ships navigating the treacherous coast. There was a time when one could even paddle up to the house in a small boat, though Hammock House is today decidedly landlocked. Constructed from sturdy Scotch heart pine and boasting the double front porch so prevalent in the architecture of the West Indies, the uniquely named Hammock House derived its name from the hammock (by definition, a fertile raised area) upon which it was built and was probably originally built to serve as an inn for travelers passing through the area by both land and sea.

Its builders were clearly concerned with sturdiness and durability, and Hammock House has little in common aesthetically with the regal and magnificent country manors and plantation homes of the Carolinas. But unlike its more attractive brethren, Hammock House, like its resident spirits, has well withstood the passage of time. It was constructed by men used to building ships and was therefore crafted lovingly to endure. Its hardy construction is plainly visible even now; many of its exterior weatherboards remain and the exposed massive pine beams, which run the entire width of the house, testify to the home's endurance. The home gained national prominence in the 1970s when Sears used the building to advertise its Weatherbeater paint, and today it boasts a lovely collection of furnishings predating the Civil War.

While the building did serve as an inn, it was also home to many of the early luminaries of Beaufort. Among them were Robert Turner, who initiated the town's layout in 1713, and Nathaniel Taylor, who donated the land that would become the Old Burying Ground. But, surprisingly, there was a time when Beaufort residents were willing to consign the historical home to the wrecking ball; long neglected and ignored, Hammock House had become a victim of its own notoriety. Accounts of its haunted past have been bandied about for almost as long as the house has stood and these stories may have contributed to the building's decline. But fortuitously, Hammock House was saved and, ironically, it might be said that it's the ghosts, to some extent, that are responsible for the house's popularity today.

Hammock House's most famous resident is also undoubtedly its most notorious. According to local folklore, Blackbeard frequented Hammock House. During one of his stays, he met a young French woman with whom he quickly became enamored. Blackbeard was alleged to have had at least a dozen wives and he meant to add this young woman to his tally. However, she had little regard for the man with the most fearsome of appearances and gamely resisted his overtures. Blackbeard, unaccustomed to such rejection, flew into a vengeful rage. Before casting off in his ship, he had the poor, wretched girl dragged, kicking and screaming, to a stand of oak trees where he placed a noose around her neck and hanged her from a branch. Her body was buried beneath the tree. Even now, on nights when the skies are clear and the moon is full, people claim that her screams can be heard once again as the girl spends an eternity fruitlessly begging for her life. At Hammock House, hers is not the only spirit to make its presence felt.

Another local ghost is that of sailor Richard Russell, Jr. On the second-floor landing of Hammock House, there is a strange stain blotting the wooden boards. It bears a marked and disturbing resemblance to a dried pool of blood. For years, people have tried washing away the stain but it always reappears. According to legend, blood was first spilled upon that spot in 1747 by Russell, Jr. The sailor had just returned from sea and decided that his first order of business was to attend to the punishment of one of his misbehaving slaves. As was his wont, Russell began leading the slave toward the attic. The slave, having once experienced the lash at his master's hands, meant not to go through it again, especially when he had no idea what he might have done to deserve such a thing. Sensing an opportunity as Russell fumbled with his keys, the slave struck his master with a hard, bony elbow to the nose, and then shoved against the stunned sailor with all of his weight. Russell tumbled down the stairs with an ugly clatter punctuated by what sounded like the snapping of bone until finally, he came to a rest on the second-floor landing, blood pooling beneath his head. Aghast, the slave fled from the house as quickly as he could and was never seen in Beaufort again. As for Russell, he died that day upon the landing, and though he was buried beneath six feet of earth, something of his soul lingers on at Hammock House in the blood stain that refuses to wash away and in the haunting presence that is often felt, if not seen, upon the second-floor landing.

Russell, of course, should not be confused with the ghost of the young adulteress that a psychic recently claimed to have seen on the second floor. Names and dates have been lost from the accounts of this particular ghost, though the setting is, without a doubt, Hammock House. When it served as an inn, Hammock House must certainly have been a more than convenient place for lovers seeking a quiet and secluded place for a clandestine meeting. It certainly proved thusly for a young woman, married just a few weeks and only at her parents' urging. She had little affection for her husband, who, despite his privileged background, was a boor and a cad. She gravitated toward the arms of another, and it wasn't long before they were meeting regularly on the second floor of Hammock House. But while the two lovers were initially cautious, as the months passed, they became careless. They stole smoldering glances at each other when they passed on the street, exchanges which did not go unnoticed. And when word reached the woman's husband that she had been seen coming and going from Hammock House on a consistent basis, he himself made a trip to the inn. The proprietor, a wad of newly acquired bills lining his greasy pockets, informed the husband which room his wife favored. With the promise of a further profit, the innkeeper vowed to alert the husband when his wife next appeared.

One cloudy day, a messenger on horseback arrived at the husband's home with the news for which he'd been waiting. His wife was at the inn, safely ensconced within a second-floor room. The husband raced off on his swiftest steed and, with the key to the room in his trembling hand, opened the door to see his wife wrapped in the warm embrace of another man, favoring him with a gaze he himself, as her husband, had never seen. With a roar, he lumbered into the room, grabbed his wife by the arm and tossed her to the floor. Her head crashed against it with a sickly thud and, with a gurgling sputter, she breathed her last breath. Her husband cast a triumphant gaze down at his wife and then walked calmly from the room. Her tragic death assured the wife a place within Hammock House's pantheon of spirits, and since that time, her mournful apparition has been seen countless times wandering the halls of the second floor, sometimes as nothing more than a wispy shadow, other times as a full-fledged apparition dressed in a gown. Hers is a staggering presence, reportedly overwhelming those near her with an oppressive sensation of sadness.

Misery and murder seem to be prerequisites for the hauntings of Hammock House, and the story of Madison Brothers is no exception. An excellent seaman blessed with a seemingly preternatural ability for business, Madison Brothers could, when calm, be a delightful presence. But, like the unpredictable waters of the Atlantic that he navigated so assuredly, Brothers possessed a temper so foul and feared that he'd acquired the moniker Captain Mad. When not at sea, Brothers called Hammock House home, and he chose it to serve as the setting for his wedding. While in Baltimore, Maryland, Brothers met and fell in love with a stunning woman named Samantha Ashby. It was almost love at first sight, and before long the two were betrothed. On the eve of her wedding, Ashby, her bridesmaids and their chaperones traveled to Beaufort by stagecoach. Brothers, of course, opted for the sea, but inclement weather delayed his arrival. When at long last he saw the glistening timbers of his freshly white-washed home along the shore, he breathed a great sigh of relief. He dropped anchor and lowered himself into his yawl. As quickly as he could, he paddled to Hammock House, which was ablaze with the festive lights of a splendid party. From Taylor's Creek, Brothers could see friends and family chatting amiably on the porch and his heart swooned thinking about his bride-to-be.

Ashore, he exchanged quick greetings with the friends gathered outside and hurried inside to greet his future wife. He looked to the top of the stairs and with a wide smile, lovingly gazed upon Ashby. Bathed in the soft flickering glow of candlelight, her beauty seemed to have increased tenfold. She had yet to see him and, with a great smile, she wrapped her arms around a strange man and accompanied the gesture with a loving peck on the stranger's cheek. Brothers watched in horror and his great temper was ignited. Captain Mad drew his sword, bounded up the steps and plunged his blade deep within the stranger's chest. Ashby screamed as the man collapsed to the floor, a red bloom blossoming across his white shirt. He stared from Ashby to Brothers in wide-eyed confusion and with his last breath, looked at a frantic Ashby and said, "Samantha?" Ashby threw herself upon his body and in a voice muffled by her sobs, cried out, "Alas, Madison! You've killed my brother!" It was, needless to say, an inauspicious start to their union. Whatever became of Captain Mad, his temper and Samantha Ashby isn't known but immortalizing the tale is the ghost of Ashby's brother, whose spirit is often seen and felt at the Hammock House. His is a gentle spirit and he seems to have adapted quite nicely to his adopted home. Though it is far from his home of Baltimore, Hammock House seems to have served the Ashby brother well as a substitute.

Given the fantastic stories originating from Hammock House, it's hard to imagine that there exists a story even more fantastic, more awesome and more fascinating. But there is just such an account and for years it has offered a mystery that perhaps will never be solved.

By the 19th century, Beaufort had evolved from a sleepy little fishing town into a well-established port city, a center for agriculture, commerce and politics and a favored spot for the wealthy to visit during the summer months. It figured prominently in the minds of Union war planners as war with the South became ever more of a reality. But unlike many of the cities of the South, ravaged and put to the torch by Federal troops bent on destruction, Beaufort emerged from the Civil War relatively unscathed. It was occupied early. When Federal soldiers arrived to take possession of Beaufort, many soldiers simply found lodgings wherever there was space to accommodate them. Hammock House was quickly appropriated to serve as lodgings. One day, three

Federal soldiers arrived at the deserted Hammock House and promptly vanished. They were never seen alive again and people whispered that the ghosts must have gotten them.

In 1915, workers were excavating the back porch of Hammock House when they made an intriguing discovery. Working carefully with trowels and brushes, they unearthed three belt buckles and buttons from Federal uniforms. Along with these metal trinkets, workers unearthed the grisly remains of three young men. One digger is said to have muttered, "Well, so that's what happened to those Yankees." Nobody knows for certain what happened to the three soldiers but the involvement of the supernatural has long been suspected. Following the end of the Civil War, Hammock House fell victim to abuse, vandalism and neglect. People whispered that the house was cursed and, well, who could really blame them for thinking so?

Of course, the people of 21st-century Beaufort, North Carolina, are not so easily cowed by such accounts. They've become accustomed to the ghosts of Hammock House and its current owners allegedly quite enjoy the added company. The odd bumps in the night, the floorboards that creak beneath invisible feet, the fleeting shadows that pass through open doorways and the bizarre sensations that come with entering certain parts of the house only add to the allure of inhabiting Beaufort's oldest house. When it was first constructed at the turn of the 18th century, Hammock House's planners clearly envisioned a building that would endure. And so it has, becoming in the process a very real part of Beaufort's past and a vessel for the colorful characters of its history.

The Harper House

The Battle of Bentonville, fought from March 19 to 21, 1865, marked the last time the Confederate Army was able to mount an offensive in the Civil War. It was the largest battle fought on North Carolina soil and is notable for being the only major Confederate attempt to bring an end to Union General William T. Sherman's march through the Carolinas.

In the spring of 1865, the Confederacy was teetering on the brink of defeat. Georgia (through which Sherman had rampaged during his March to the Sea) and South Carolina lay in smoldering ruins. The Army of Tennessee and other Confederate forces in the Carolinas were scattered throughout the South. Confederate General Robert E. Lee's once-mighty Army of Northern Virginia was mired in a struggle against Union General Ulysses S. Grant at Petersburg, Virginia, desperate to hold onto the city of Richmond. Union General Sherman and 60,000 of his Federal troops were in North Carolina, swiftly marching north from Fayetteville, seeking to enter Virginia and join General Grant to deliver the fatal blow.

Sherman had to be stopped, and the daunting task fell to Confederate General Joseph E. Johnston, commander of all Confederate forces from Florida to North Carolina. His forces numbered only 20,000 but times were desperate and the situation was dire. His forces took up positions around Bentonville and on the morning of March 19, they encountered Union troops.

The Battle of Bentonville was fought over an area of 6000 acres that was mostly pine woods and fields. By the end, as

Union General William T. Sherman

the Confederates slinked away defeated, 543 men lay dead,
with over 28,000 wounded and 900 missing. Confederate
General Johnston had failed miserably. Sherman joined
Grant at Petersburg, breaking the stalemate, and the Union
took Richmond, Virginia, on April 3. The war in the Carolinas
continued for another month after Bentonville but the

Confederates had been broken. On April 26, at Bennett Place near Durham, Confederate General Johnston surrendered his army and the war came to an end in the Carolinas, Florida and Georgia.

On the first day of the battle, Union troops occupied a small, quaint two-story home with white walls and black trim for use as a field hospital. It belonged to John and Amy Harper, and by the end of the battle, over 500 soldiers, including 45 Confederates, were treated at the makeshift facility. Throughout the bloody three-day battle, John and Amy Harper and their seven children remained at the home, tending to the wounded. Today the grounds of the Battle of Bentonville are a North Carolina Historic Site and include the restored Harper House.

The downstairs rooms of Harper House have been restored to represent a Civil War field hospital, while the upstairs rooms reflect the everyday life of the Harpers. It is a popular stop for visitors arriving to tour the battlefield. Within its walls lurk the restless spirits of those fallen men who died in combat so long ago, as well as the compassionate Harpers themselves.

According to local folklore, in 1905 two hunters were in the woods near Harper House when they witnessed the Battle of Bentonville being fought once more, not by re-enactors, but by the ghostly soldiers themselves. One of the hunters was a man named Jim Weaver. He was a farmer and a miller, known to friends as the "Blue Man." His skin had a blue pallor, common to users of the silver nitrate then prescribed to sufferers of epilepsy. Late one March evening, he and a friend, Joe Lewis, were out hunting possums. His hound ran into a thicket and began barking loudly. The two hunters followed quickly, knowing that the dog had treed a possum.

Brandishing his ax, Weaver began chopping at the tree's trunk. When the blade cut deep into the bark, a blinding flash exploded in the skies above. Weaver let go of his ax and watched, frightened, as night turned to day. One flash followed another, erupting in the thick stands of pine and casting ethereal shadows. Silhouetted against these bright explosions, figures clad in the uniforms of Union and Confederate soldiers ran through the trees brandishing muskets fixed with bayonets.

The ground began to shake, and Weaver and Lewis, cowering in abject fear, heard the thundering of hundreds of hooves. They dove to the ground as the ghostly cavalry thundered over them. The air was rent with the crack and pop of musket fire and the whistle of bullets whizzing around them. Soldiers fell to the ground, their bodies contorted into grotesque poses. Men stabbed blindly with their bayonets, impaling friend and foe alike. Weaver watched in horror as a Union soldier, who couldn't have been older than 17, wrestled with the flag bearer of a Confederate unit. Another Confederate rushed to the aid of his companion and was promptly run through by the Union soldier's bayonet. The Confederate watched as a fountain of blood erupted from his companion's throat and in that moment he was stabbed in the shoulder with a knife. He fell to the ground in agony.

Weaver and Lewis had had enough and, having recovered some of their senses, began to run from the scene. When they passed the Harper House, its panes were illuminated by great balls of flame, and a strange light emanated from within.

They didn't stop running until they reached Weaver's log cabin, where they collapsed on the ground, exhausted.

Days later, Weaver spoke with the battle's survivors and was able to describe, with frightening accuracy, details of the conflict. The veterans were said to have marveled at how true his account of the Battle of Bentonville had been, but none more so than a veteran in his 50s who listened with a shudder. His left arm hung limp and useless at his side. In 1865, the veteran had been only 17 and he fought alongside his brother. During the Battle of Bentonville, he'd been given the duty of carrying his unit's standard. He had thought it was quite an honor until he encountered the Union soldier who impaled his brother and then stabbed him in his shoulder. Years later the battlefield is still reportedly haunted. So, too, is Harper House.

Harper House has a security system, but to date there has only been one attempted break-in and it was a spectacular failure. Two would-be thieves broke into the home and immediately realized that they had made a terrible mistake. The air in the house was terribly cold, which was odd considering that the air conditioning was never used at night. As they made their way through the home, the thieves came to the startling conclusion that they weren't alone. Heavy footsteps from the upper floor reverberated throughout the home, pacing back and forth across the floor and then approaching the landing at the top of the staircase. The thieves turned on their flashlights and haltingly panned their beams up to the landing. Standing there glowering fiercely down at them with his stern, deep-set eyes was the specter of the long-dead John Harper. The thieves dropped whatever they had collected and fled through the front door. As they

In 1905 two hunters witnessed the Battle of Bentonville fought by ghostly soldiers.

ran across the field, they distinctly heard the door being slammed shut.

A short time later, the two men approached a police officer in a nearby town, admitting, wild-eyed and terrified, to their crime. These hardened men sought now only to repent, and at their trial the local prosecutor asked for only the minimum sentence. He felt, as the would-be robbers did, that the two men had surely learned their lesson and would never again enter where they were not welcome. Harper House has a way of resurrecting the past so that it's rendered immediate and visceral.

One former employee of Harper House was working alone on a cold and rainy morning. With a start, he turned his head toward the second story from where he had heard heavy, plodding footsteps. The employee gingerly walked up the stairs and conducted a thorough search of the second-floor rooms. He found nothing amiss. He was, it appeared, still alone. Shaking his head, he walked back down the staircase and was starting down the central hallway when he heard a shuffling that seemed to come from the landing at the top of the staircase. For a moment he paused, not wanting to look up, terrified by the idea of what he just might see there. But, like Lot's wife at Sodom, curiosity got the better of him and he looked back. A dark apparition stood at the top of the stairs. The employee turned and bolted from the house, refusing to be alone in it ever again.

One of the more interesting stories concerning the spirits of Harper House is that of a tour group and one particularly sensitive psychic. The group arrived from Manassas, Virginia, and in an unusual move went directly to Harper House. Most groups tended to start at the site's Visitor Center before moving on. During the guided tour of the home, a woman began experiencing visions from the past.

As the group moved through the upstairs bedrooms and its collection of period artifacts, the woman stopped short. The guide noticed her shock and asked her what was wrong. "Don't you see him?" the woman asked. Everyone in the room followed the woman's gaze but saw nothing except a window. "What are you seeing?" the guide asked. The woman began to describe how she saw a tall figure standing in front of the window. His lanky frame was draped in a long black coat, offset by a full white beard and stern, deep-set eyes. His eyebrows were coarse, thick and dark. He seemed transfixed by something out in the yard below. People in the group nudged each other with nervous laughter, not quite sure what to do. After all, none of them saw anything unusual.

Gingerly, the guide continued the tour. They left the house and on the porch, the psychic woman again saw the mysterious figure. As the tour continued on the grounds of the Bentonville battlefield, the woman, like the two hunters before her, saw the Battle of Bentonville re-enacted. She saw horse-drawn ambulances pulling up to the house and soldiers with gaping wounds and severed limbs lying on their litters. Dead soldiers lay stacked like firewood in the yard. Attendants rushed from Harper House to carry the wounded inside where sand and sawdust covered the floor to sop up the blood and steady the legs of the field surgeons. She heard the agonizing screams of dying men and witnessed the steady compassion of John and Amy Harper as they wandered from one dying patient to the next, administering kind words and smiles in a task that must surely have struck them as Sisyphean though necessary.

The woman also reported seeing a wounded Union general come to the hospital for treatment. The man was bleeding heavily from the side and he clutched one hand tightly in a blood-soaked rag. It must surely have been Brigadier General Benjamin D. Fearing, the only Union general known to have been wounded during the Battle of Bentonville. During his counterattack on March 19, Fearing was shot in the side and a bullet shattered several fingers on one hand. He was brought to Harper House for treatment.

The guide then knew that the woman must surely be blessed with extrasensory perception. How could the woman have described in such exacting detail the injuries Brigadier General Fearing had suffered on that terrible day? The guide knew the stories of the Battle of Bentonville well, but such were the demands of her job. This woman from Manassas, who had never visited Bentonville before, was too precise, too specific not to be believed. The description of the thin figure in the house could have been none other than John Harper, but the guide kept quiet. She would lead the group to the Visitor Center where they would see a photograph of the man. She wanted to see how the woman would react.

When the group entered the Visitor Center, the woman gasped. "That's him," she said breathlessly as she pointed at a sepia-toned photograph of a man with a long thin nose; his face was weary and taut, his eyes set in an almost mournful and exhausted gaze and his mouth fixed with a tight frown atop a brilliant white bushy beard. "That's the man I saw in the house!" She walked over to the picture and saw that it was none other than John Harper. It was by far one of the most memorable and bizarre tours given at Bentonville.

The Civil War left the United States psychically scarred and battered. In North Carolina, nowhere are the aftershocks of the great conflict felt more keenly than at Bentonville. Though the site today is verdant and serene, the spirits of soldiers tossed into the cauldron of war fight on. And John Harper continues to stand as a silent witness, his grim and haggard visage a heartbreaking and devastating testament to the horrors of war.

2

Haunted Railroads

The Maco Light

In 1888, Grover Cleveland sought a second term as president of the United States, and he took his message to the people. The presidential train snaked its way lazily through the mists and fogs of the North Carolina countryside along the Atlantic Coast Line Railroad, which stretched from Augusta to Wilmington. Inside, Cleveland kept a watchful eye upon the darkness that covered the land. The train was approaching Maco, a speck of a town with few living denizens but one particularly restive ghost. Cleveland had heard the stories of the Maco Light and was eager to see it for himself.

The conductor walked through the carriage, announcing that Wilmington station was the next stop. Cleveland peered out his window eagerly. At first, he saw nothing unusual and his hopes flagged. But then, he watched with great surprise as what he could only describe as a flickering ball of light passed by his window before crashing to the ground and flaming out into the pitch. Intrigued, Cleveland called the conductor over and told him about what he had seen. "You've just seen the Maco Light, Mr. President," the conductor answered. With a sly smile, he began to tell Cleveland the story of Joe Baldwin, the unfortunate railroad flagman whose otherwise unremarkable life had quickly become the stuff of legend. Maco locals knew all too well about Joe Baldwin and his death; when they weren't talking about it, they were headed for the tracks, wondering what they might see this time.

It all began in 1867. Joe worked for the Atlantic Coast Line Railroad as a flagman, the brakeman at the rear end of the train. He had worked this line for years, tuned in to the rhythms of the terrain that rushed by him. It was dangerous work, and though he never scoffed at the risks he took, he trusted his experience, his knowledge and his muscled arms. He spent part of every shift on the roof of the train, turning those great metal wheels with precision to bring the train to a steady stop. Turning them too much could grind a wheel, rubbing a flat spot into the metal and taking $45, his month's pay, out of his pocket. It had yet to happen. Even on this night, with the rain cascading down in great undulating sheets, he navigated the roofs with a steady step.

As he looked out into the rain, he could see the lights of Maco in the distance. *It's time*, he told himself. Time to announce Wilmington. In a few minutes, he would be home, in bed with his wife. He entered the empty rear coach and made his way to the passenger cars. As he approached the door, he knew something was wrong. The cabin seemed to be slowing down. He flung open the door and immediately saw why. Somehow, this last coach, the coach he was riding in, had come unhitched from the rest of the train. He watched with a frown as the train pulled away, its lights fading into the distance. Only then did he remember that there had been another train following close behind.

Joe grabbed his kerosene lantern and hurried to the rear of the cabin. He had to make sure the approaching train stopped in time. Already, he could feel its rumble beneath his suddenly unsteady legs. He stood outside, waving his lantern to and fro, hoping that somehow the engineer would be able to see his beacon in the rain. Unfortunately, he didn't. The train crashed into the solitary car, reducing it to splinters and twisted hulks of metal. Joe's decapitated body was tossed from the car. His lantern soared through the air, end over end, before it crashed pitifully into the woods. Authorities never did find Joe's head.

The stories began not long after service along the railroad resumed. Train engineers reported stopping their trains just outside of Maco because of a bright white light they assumed came from the flagman of a train in front of them. When they set out to investigate, they found nothing but two empty lengths of track stretching toward the horizon. The sightings became so frequent that administrators of the Atlantic Coast Line Railroad were forced to adopt colored lanterns, one red and one green, so that they might distinguish them from what was quickly becoming known as the Maco Light.

Locals became convinced that the mysterious light was Joe Baldwin, reincarnated in spectral and luminescent form. Was he looking for his head? Or was he still trying to warn other locomotives of his solitary and stranded coach? It didn't really matter. The light became famous, and everyone offered an opinion as to its cause and meaning. Some even believed that it was the spirit of a fallen Native American warrior.

After the mysterious beam was reported in newspapers, the Maco Light quickly became one of the most popular phenomena in North Carolina. Accounts of experiences became commonplace as thousands of people trekked to Maco with hopes of glimpsing the light. The number of skeptics grew too, and many claimed that the Maco Light could be the spontaneous combustion of swamp gas, or perhaps just the reflection of automobile headlights. Of course, Joe Baldwin's death had come at a time when the automobile had yet to populate the American landscape.

In 1925, two farm boys sought out the light and got more than they wanted when the light allegedly chased them for miles into the woods. Decades later, a World War II veteran, familiar with fear and panic, found himself fleeing down the tracks because he thought the light was pursuing him. With the increased popularity of the automobile, the Maco tracks became a popular destination not just for the young and adventurous, but also for families.

Tia Wernick was only six years old in 1963, but she still remembers in great detail the night she and her family went to see the Maco Light. "I had heard of it," she recalls, "but I had no idea that it might be associated with a ghost." As a child, Wernick was skeptical of the existence of the paranormal and her parents had cautioned her brother not to reveal the history behind the Maco Light. "I suppose they thought I'd be terrified," she says, "and I probably would have been. It's a pretty gruesome story."

So, blissfully ignorant, Wernick went with her family to Maco Station from their home in nearby Wilmington. When they arrived, the Wernicks saw that they were not the only ones with that idea in mind. "There were about 15 other cars there," Wernick says, "all lined up alongside the tracks." Wernick, already excited enough, could barely contain her anticipation. The sight of the other cars, each carrying their own expectant passengers, only served to heighten the mood. She didn't have to wait long.

"Soon, it all began," she remembers, the nostalgia clear in her voice. "The light appeared. It came down the tracks— very, very slowly—and it swayed from side to side. Like someone was swinging it. And then, it flipped into the air, going end over end, and then once it hit the woods, it just

Locals became convinced that the mysterious light was Joe Baldwin, reincarnated in spectral and luminescent form.

went out. Like the lamp had shattered or something." That was the beginning of Wernick's long relationship with the light. She has seen it so often that she has become an expert of sorts, able, with little prodding, to recall anecdotes she's heard about the lights over the years.

Take the time, for example, that her brother stood on the tracks watching the light drift slowly toward him. The light got closer and closer; so close that he thought he could reach out and touch it. It then just disappeared, only to reappear seconds later behind him. She recalls another incident with amusement: two young boys, intent on capturing the light, chased it around with a butterfly net. It seemed as if the light had a will of its own; it slowed down, allowed the boys to catch up and then, at the very last moment, darted off once more. The boys, their optimism and enthusiasm unbent, continued their hapless pursuit.

The light proved so reliable that it quickly became a favorite stop on the Wernick tour of North Carolina. Whenever family or friends came to visit, a trip to Maco was sure to be in the offing. No one went away disappointed; even the most skeptical of Wernick's aunts, uncles and cousins went away slack-jawed. For Wernick, the light has the same effect on her now as it did when she was just six years old. "It's still something magical," she says.

Wernick's fondest memory of the Maco Light is of one of the last times she saw it. It was 1973. Wernick was 17 and, like many young couples from Wilmington, she and her boyfriend often drove down the highway to Maco. Once they reached the little side road near the station, they parked the car and walked along the tracks until they reached a trestle. They sat down, one couple among many, to watch and wait.

"I saw it in the distance," Wernick says. "It flickered into being as if someone had struck a match." As before, the light swayed from one side to the other, increasing in speed and frequency until you could almost see Joe Baldwin resurrected once more. Wernick, never having approached the light before, did so on this night. She swears that she got close enough to see the frame of the lantern, fastenings and all. The light then arced through the air, as it was wont to do, and flickered out. Wernick could only whisper, "Wow." As she began walking back down the tracks with her boyfriend, she suddenly felt very cold. "It was the oddest thing," Wernick recalls. "It was a hot summer night, and if you've ever experienced a summer night in North Carolina, you know it's going to be hot and muggy. But there I was, freezing. And then, just like that, it was gone." The boyfriend showed no signs of having experienced the same thing until she asked. He didn't say much, but the fear in his eyes said everything. Wernick and her boyfriend hurried back to the car and drove away. "I wasn't scared at all," Wernick boasts, "but he was just terrified."

That experience preceded a spell of increasingly unsuccessful trips to Maco. Wernick no longer saw the light regularly. Between 1975 and 1977, Wernick admits to making at least 10 trips to Maco, each one as fruitless as the last. She determined that the light's scarcity of appearances must have had something to do with the state's expansion of Highway 74/76, which ran parallel to the tracks. "With the expansion, the cars ran a lot closer to the tracks," she explains. "Maybe that had something to do with it." In 1977, the tracks were torn up and it seemed as if Baldwin's spirit had been taken with them.

Today, weeds choke the empty railroad bed. The once-popular trestle is gone; nothing is left now but a few sickly stumps of rotten wood sticking out from the water. People coming to see the Maco Light leave in awe, not of the spirit of Joe Baldwin, but of the hordes of gigantic mosquitoes. For Wernick, the absence of the Maco Light is somewhat tragic. "So much about that light reminds me of my childhood," she laments. "Now, everything is gone. The tracks, the trestle, it's all gone. I suppose you never can go back."

There are those in Maco who still remember the Maco Light, but now many neither recall the phenomenon nor know the story of Joe Baldwin. Still, hundreds of people make the trip to the little town that once sat next to the Atlantic Coast Line Railroad, ever hopeful that Joe Baldwin will make his appearance.

The Pactolus Light

For students of East Carolina University, life in Greenville, North Carolina—or, as they call it, G-Vegas—can sometimes use a little spicing up (the city has proclaimed itself the "Hammock-making Capital of the World"). Some students snag fake IDs and spend their nights roaming the hangouts of Greenville Boulevard, and some while away their free time watching the ECU Pirates play football. But for the adventurous and curious, it has long been popular to seek out the Pactolus Light. Indeed, there was a time when students seeking to join one of ECU's many sororities or fraternities were pretty much assured a trip to Pactolus.

Pactolus was a small river in the ancient country of Lydia, and was famed for its gold-rich waters. Pactolus is now also a small town in Pitt County, North Carolina, which long ago failed to live up to its bountiful name. Still, its lure is undeniable, and it can all be traced back to an early 20th-century story of love, tragedy and misfortune.

The specifics of the story have been lost in the passage of time, but enough of the account remains to stir the heart. In the early years of the 20th century, a young Greenville man enrolled at a teacher-training school in Greenville (which later became East Carolina University). He met a young woman, and they quickly fell in love. When the school term ended, she had to return to her home in Richmond County. With a heavy heart, she bade goodbye to her love and promised to return in the fall.

For four months, the smitten couple wrote letters, imagining how wonderful life would be when they were reunited.

They shared their hopes and dreams, and the man, certain now that he had met his future wife, concocted a plan to propose to her. He knew that the train she would be taking back to Greenville would have to stop at Pactolus, so he would ride from Greenville to meet her there.

On the appointed day, he rode to Pactolus upon a magnificent steed. In his pocket, he carried the ring, which, if everything worked out, she would be wearing by the end of the day. Though his horse remained earthbound, his soul and spirit soared. He could hardly contain his anticipation.

He arrived early at the Pactolus train station and sat down. He waited. And waited. And waited. Afternoon turned to dusk, and evening followed. His love's train had been delayed. With a frown and a sigh, the young man returned to his saddle, spurred his horse and turned back toward Greenville. His solitary progress, however, did not pass unnoticed. In the dark, three pairs of eyes watched him, the young man's great stallion too grand a temptation for their avaricious hearts to resist. Such a horse would fetch a handsome prize and they meant to claim it. Using the shadows and bushes as cover, the men waited and watched as the young man drew closer. When they felt he was close enough, the three men leapt out from hiding, falling upon the young man and his horse.

One would like to imagine that the young man fought dearly for his life and that he might have even escaped, but it was not to be. The young man was torn from his saddle and overwhelmed as he lay helpless on the ground. His lifeless body was cast into the thick undergrowth that lined the railroad tracks. The horse proved a far more elusive prey. It ran off down the tracks, tossing off its assailants as if they were nothing more than horseflies.

A few days later, the weary horse returned to the young man's home. The family, already fearing the worst when their son failed to return as planned with his love, was devastated when the horse returned without its rider. The young woman had arrived only recently, and the luggage in her arms was far lighter than the burden her broken heart would now have to bear. Though a search for the young man was carried out, it was fruitless. He was nowhere to be found.

Not long after, whispered rumors surfaced of a eerie light roaming the tracks at the Pactolus train station. Those who heard the story were convinced that the young man's spirit had returned, determined to meet his love's train.

For almost a century, the Pactolus Light has proven fascinating. It quickly became a cornerstone of fraternity and sorority initiations of nearby East Carolina University. For years, pledges have taken Highway 264 East out of Greenville, then driven down Highway 30 and onto the dirt road named "Carl Morris." The tracks of the Pactolus train station once ran near this desolate stretch of road, now rutted and treacherous. The railroad ties are long gone, with nothing but a deep path to mark their former existence.

Once there, pleges must follow precise instructions to summon the young man's spirit. They flash their car headlights three times in quick succession and wait for the Pactolus Light to reveal itself. Often, it does.

Cody Leto (name has been changed to protect sources' identities) remembers hearing about the Pactolus Light from a friend in his dorm when he was a freshman at East Carolina University in 1989. Intrigued, he persuaded a few of his friends to drive out with him, just to see if the story was in any way true.

They drove out to Pactolus but found the dirt path impassable in their car. Rains had turned the lane into a mud bowl. They proceeded on foot and, after walking about a mile, reached the area the light is known to illuminate. Of course, without their car, they couldn't flash its lights three times. Instead, they began beating on the tracks and yelling obscenities; apparently, the spirit of the young man reacts to such stimuli as well. As the last of their voices died out, they sat down to wait. Like the young man long before them, they waited and waited. Nothing happened. They sat on the tracks for the better part of an hour before they grew weary of their own conversation and began walking back toward their car. As is so often the case, they happened to wait just long enough.

As they walked, Leto spotted something in the distance. "It was a light," he says, "just down the path, hovering above the ground. It looked like a car with one broken headlight or something." The light then dropped and, after a few breathless moments, it began to move toward them. "It was so bright," Leto says. "And huge. I mean, it was huge." It accelerated, and Leto and his friends ran, their collective curiosity now replaced by fear. They ran and ran, and could see their car just ahead of them when the light vanished as inexplicably as it had appeared.

Leto's account resembles those of dozens of others. Witnesses have often seen the solitary light hover above the ground, about the height of a man riding a horse, before dropping to the ground, as if the rider has dismounted. In one aspect, however, Leto's experience is different. Few have seen the light charge; in fact, more often than not, anyone who approaches the orb will spook the ghostly young man's horse, sending the light fleeing down the path.

This happened to Sofia Knop and her boyfriend a few years ago. "I was from Pactolus," Sofia states, "and I had seen a great deal of strange things. He didn't believe a word of what I'd told him and, well, I guess I proved him wrong." They headed for the secluded path and sat down to wait. "I heard about all those things: flashing headlights and swearing. But I've never had to do any of those things to see the light."

Sofia and her boyfriend hadn't been sitting long when she glimpsed the appearance of a small orange light. She nudged her boyfriend, who watched, transfixed, as it turned from orange to a brilliant white. The light began to approach and Sofia laughed as her boyfriend shut his eyes tightly. "He was terrified," Sofia says, laughing. "The big boy was absolutely scared." She nudged him again, then whispered, "Watch this." She stood up and approached the light. The light fled from her. "I wish I'd brought a video camera," she laments. "The look on his face was priceless." Sofia and her boyfriend plan on returning to Pactolus sometime soon, determined to capture the Pactolus Light on tape. It may be a tall order.

As fascinating as the phenomenon is, sightings of the light are becoming rare, though this has little to do with the light itself. The property on which the light appears is now privately owned, and its owners would much prefer that trespassers stay far, far away. To that end, a mound of dirt now squats in the middle of the old railroad bed, ready to thwart any vehicle short of a tank from venturing farther. Some intrepid ghost hunters have reported being chased from the property by men in pickup trucks, weary of the sort of curiosity seekers and bored teens that such phenomena seem to draw. The lovestruck young man, however, will most likely roam the land for many more years to come.

Vander Light

It was late and ticket master Archer Matthews was very tired. From the shelter of the Vander train station, he peered out into the darkness, weary of both the job and the rain that had fallen since morning. His lantern cast hardly enough feeble light to beat back the night. He pulled his overcoat tighter around his body, his joints stiff with the cold. He checked his pocket watch and shook it to make sure it was still working. It was. He sighed and then frowned. The train was late.

He pulled out his pouch of tobacco and rolled himself a cigarette. He inhaled deeply, already feeling a little calmer. From beyond the tracks, a strange rattling sound caught Matthews' attention. Raising his lantern, Matthews stepped to the edge of the platform to see what was out there. Seeing nothing but drops of rain that passed like sparks through the beam of his lantern, Matthews leaned over the edge. The rain that had been falling for hours had soaked the platform, making it slick. Matthews pitched forward and, during the second it took him to fall to the tracks, cursed himself for his stupidity. And then everything went black.

The train engineer muttered darkly to himself, urging the train forward. He was already half an hour late. Archer Matthews wouldn't be happy. With a smile and a sigh of relief, the engineer realized that the Vander Station was near. Slowing the train, he peered out beyond the rain-spattered window and uttered a quiet prayer of thanks. The station was dark, meaning that there were no passengers waiting to board his empty train. He could just coast by and finally start making up some lost time. The train picked up speed once

The train squealed in protest as its wheels ground against the tracks.

again and drew ever closer to where ticket master Archer Matthews lay unconscious on the tracks.

The train engineer frowned. What was that curious light on the tracks? Squinting, the engineer craned his neck forward trying to get a better look. With a start, he realized what it was. It was Matthews' lantern, and lying there, wanly illuminated in its smoky, feeble glow, was a body. The engineer cursed loudly and applied the brakes to the locomotive. *Please stop*, he prayed urgently. *Please stop in time.* The train squealed in protest, its metal wheels sending out a shower of sparks as they ground against the tracks. *Too late,* the engineer told himself. *It's too late.* He closed his eyes as the train roared past Vander Station. The engineer didn't even feel a thing as the locomotive ground Archer Matthews into a pulp beneath its wheels.

When the train finally did come to a stop, the engineer hurried back to Vander Station as quickly as he could. The lantern lay in the middle of the tracks, untouched and still casting its light. In the half circle of its light lay Archer Matthews, whose face looked surprisingly peaceful, as if he'd only crawled out onto the tracks to take a nap. The rest of him was a gnarled, twisted mess. The mere sight of it sent convulsions through the engineer, and he vomited then promptly fainted.

This gruesome accident occurred some time in the 18th century near Vander, a speck of a community in Cumberland County, North Carolina. Not long after, the people in the area began seeing a strange phenomenon, which is known today as the Vander Light.

The Vander Light has often been overlooked in favor of its more celebrated and famous cousin, the Maco Light. But for the Vander locals, Archer Matthews continues to provoke fascination. The Vander Station has long since been demolished in the name of efficiency and progress, leaving a small, weed-choked clearing in its wake. Long after the fateful tracks upon which he dashed his skull fell into disuse and disrepair, Archer Matthews perseveres. Late at night, when the skies are moonless and the land is dark, Matthews emerges. Well, not Matthews exactly. Look down the old railroad tracks and two dim orbs of light may flicker into being above the tracks. One is much larger and brighter than the other. Watch for a moment and both of them will fall to the ground, then the smaller ball of light will extinguish itself. The other lolls on the tracks for a moment before winking out. People say it's Matthews with his lantern raised high in one hand and a lit cigarette in the other, once again peering over the edge of the platform and falling onto the tracks below.

Arthur Burris, who grew up in Cumberland County in the 1980s, remembers the Vander Light well, but he asked that his real name not be used in this account. "I've only seen it a couple of times," he states. The first time, Burris had gone out to the tracks alone, eager to see for himself if the stories he had heard were true. "Oh yeah," he recalls. "All us kids growing up knew about the Vander Light. It was one of those [things] you talked about in the playground or at sleepovers when you're trying to scare the bejeesus out of your friends with that flashlight under your chin." Burris recalls not being disappointed when he began walking along the tracks. He was alone with two lengths of track stretching toward the horizon in either direction. Weeds lined the rail beds and off in the distance, he could hear the bloated croaking of frogs calling out from the nearby swamp. "It's a pretty eerie place," Burris says. He pauses as if reflecting upon his memories, then laughs and continues. "Or maybe I just imagined it all."

As the skies began to darken, Burris felt a chill ripple through his body. He shivered and, drawing his coat tighter around his body, continued to walk down the tracks to where Vander Station once stood. Once there, he began to wait. He hadn't been there long when he saw a light materialize.

"It wasn't really bright and not too big," he describes. "It was kind of a brownish yellow color. Looked kind of sickly, actually." He couldn't see the cigarette that Matthews is alleged to carry, so he approached the light gingerly, never taking his eyes off it. "Then I saw it," he says. "It was a little bigger than your normal cigarette, but it looked just like the cherry of a cigarette. It was orange and red, flecked with ash, and I swear, you could see it brighten and then dim as if the guy had just taken a drag. I didn't see him exhale though." Intrigued, Burris dared to draw ever closer.

"I think I scared him, or maybe got in his line of sight," he says. When Burris approached almost close enough to touch the lights with an outstretched hand, both surprisingly winked out. Burris stood for a second, disappointed, and then suddenly felt as if he were being watched. He wheeled around. There, behind him, were the two balls of light. "I think I jumped out of my skin a little," Burris admits with a laugh. The lights lingered above the ground for a moment and then fell. Burris claims he could almost hear Matthews collapse on the tracks, the ssshh of Matthews' cigarette extinguishing itself in a puddle and the clatter of the lantern as it rolled around on the tracks. "It was something I'll never forget," Burris says.

Of course, whenever spectral lights are reported, the skeptics are never far behind. As always, people seeking a scientific and earthbound explanation point to the swamp that lies near the tracks. They claim that the Vander Light is nothing more fascinating than the will o' the wisp, the most common name for the mysterious light phenomenon that often led travelers astray and into treacherous marshes.

Scientists claim the will o' the wisp is nothing more than the oxidation of hydrogen phosphide and methane gases, which are produced by the decay of organic material common to most swamps and marshes and which cause eerie lights to appear in the air. Others posit that these mysterious lights are generated by tectonic strain, which causes the earth to heat and any water present to vaporize. Then, piezoelectric rocks, among them stones like quartz, produce an electric charge that works its way up through the earth along the column of vaporized water. When the charge reaches the surface, it reveals itself as a light. Neither explanation can offer a reason for how spectral lights like the Vander Light can bob and swoop and move independent of the wind.

Burris dismisses these explanations with a cluck of his tongue. "I don't question the existence of phenomena like will o' the wisp and St. Elmo's Fire," he says, "but if you've ever seen the Vander Light, you'd know—I mean, really know—that it's got nothing to do with methane or tectonic strains. I've seen it twice. It's Archer Matthews. That much I know."

The Vander Light, unlike the Maco Light, is still reported to appear, and it seems that in all likelihood, Archer Matthews will spend many years to come peering into the darkness before slipping off the platform to his untimely and unfortunate death.

Shoo-fly Ghost Train

On the morning of November 6, 1906, the Shoo Fly train, bound from Norfolk for Wilmington, was nearing the community of Warsaw. It never reached its destination. With a wrenching sound that split the air, the train lurched off the tracks, its cars twisting and turning through the air in a grotesque marriage of physics and momentum. It crashed along an embankment and as steam continued to belch from the engine, passengers in the Pullman cars screamed for help. Those who could free themselves quickly dedicated themselves to the rescue of others. Frantically, they tore through one piece of baggage after another, desperate to reach the baggage master, whose agonizing screams had galvanized even the most terrified into action. When at least they reached him, they were too late. The crash had broken the baggage master's back. Rescuers turned their attention to the engine car where all was silent except for the sputtering of broken pipes and the hiss of steam. The engineer and fireman were both dead; they had been scalded to death. Miraculously, not one of the train's passengers had been killed. In the resulting inquiry, investigators discovered that the accident had been a tragic convergence of fate and misfortune.

The day before the Shoo-Fly careened off the tracks, a northbound freight train stopped near Warsaw to pick up timber from a sawmill. As it pulled from the siding, its last flat car, from which protruded a lone piece of lumber, hit the main line track switch and opened it. The following day the switch was still open, and when the southbound Shoo-Fly hit the open switch at full speed, disaster was all but assured. In

Residents living near Warsaw report that the Shoo-Fly train is still determined to reach Wilmington.

a tragic coincidence, the engineer of the freight train had been a man named Will Horne. His father, Gilbert Horne, had been the engineer of the Shoo-Fly.

For years now, residents living near Warsaw report that the Shoo-Fly is still very much determined to make it to Wilmington. Nancy Roberts describes the McCauleys' 1906 experience with the Shoo-Fly ghost train. Mrs. McCauley worked at a hotel in Warsaw and each night when her shift was over, her family would be waiting for her; together they would walk back down the tracks to their home. One distinctly chilly November evening, the McCauleys were walking along the trestle leading toward their home. They were startled from their conversation by the ear-splitting whistle of an approaching train. Standing there, on the trestle, with nowhere to go but down or across, the McCauleys turned and saw behind them the approaching train, its blinding headlight growing ever larger. The McCauleys turned back and ran, gasping and panting, down the trestle. They made it across the trestle and waited to watch the train pass. The horn sounded again but as they watched, the train just vanished into the darkness. There had been no train at all.

Train engineers seeing the train often cursed in terror as their northbound cars seemed destined to collide with the southbound train, which refused to slow. With a shudder and the screech of the brakes straining against the train's momentum, the train would come to a sudden stop. Rail men would jump quickly from the train only to discover that there had been no train ahead of them.

Even now, people still have stories to tell of the Shoo-Fly ghost train, destined, it seems, to spend eternity trying to reach its destination.

Bostian Bridge

The day was hot and muggy, the air thick and heavy. Statesville men, women and children walked slowly beneath their parasols, the scant shade hardly enough to beat back the sweat that ran in rivulets down their necks and set their skin glistening beneath the torturous afternoon sun. Baggage master H.K. Linster lifted off his cap, rubbed his brow with a handkerchief and then resumed directing the porters stowing away the luggage grateful passengers had wearily deposited at their feet. Linster watched the families with envy. The train was bound for Asheville and the cooling breezes of the Blue Mountains, but unlike these passengers, he'd have to get right back on the train, baking in his starchy uniform, and head straight back into the heat that seemed to be borne straight from the furnaces of hell.

With a sigh, he stepped up into the train. No sense in despairing now, he told himself. His retirement was fast approaching. He had spent the last 30 years working the railroad, and within weeks he would be finished. With his right hand, he fingered the cool, smooth surface of his gold pocket watch and smiled. He'd only received it a few days earlier, a present from the railroad company for his dedicated years of service. The gold watch had lifted his stature and added a spring to his gait. It represented his future: the anticipated time when he, too, could set his luggage down on the platform, take a seat up in the passenger cabin with all the swells and ride in comfort to Asheville.

The train blew its whistle and began chugging its way from Statesville. Linster pulled out his watch to check the time. He frowned. The dial read half past nine, but that couldn't be right. He shook it against his ear, and with a sigh, began winding it again. He walked through the cabin, stopping next to a well-appointed family to ask them the time. "It's coming on three o'clock in the afternoon, sir," the man answered. With a nod, Linster thanked him and began to set his clock. He never finished.

With a jolt, Linster was thrown from his feet and as he fell, he watched in horror as passengers around him toppled and lurched from their seats. Bowlers and derbies flitted through the air; china teacups and silverware clattered down in a cacophonous shower. Men, women and children hung from their seats; others collided with a terrible crash against the cabin door. As Linster slid toward the door, he struggled to look out the window and saw to his horror the Bostian Bridge above and the vast emptiness of a 90-foot drop below. The train had derailed. Linster smiled to himself, surprised at how calm he was as he stared certain death in the face. "How appropriate," he murmured quietly, "how utterly ironic." He palmed the gold pocket watch and closed his eyes. The train smashed into the earth.

The following morning, August 27, 1891, the people of Statesville awoke to the news of the terrible disaster that had taken place on the Bostian Bridge out on Buffalo Shoals Road. Over 100 people had plummeted along with the train off the bridge but, as if by some miracle, 70 managed to survive. Among the 30 who lay dead was baggage master H.K. Linster. When they found him, he looked as if he'd just drifted off to sleep. His face was calm and there was even the hint of a smile tugging at the corner of his lips. Coroners determined that he'd died immediately; his neck had been snapped. One hand clutched the gold watch, its hands approaching three o'clock in the afternoon, just moments before the derailment.

The spectacular accident drew national attention. Images of the wreck could be found splashed across newspaper pages from San Francisco to Chicago to New York City. It was all anyone in Statesville could talk about, and even years later, residents could recall what they had been doing when they heard about the disaster. Families did what they could to put the wreck behind them, but its memory refused to die.

Exactly one year later, on August 26, people walking around three in the afternoon near the tracks that crossed Bostian Bridge returned to Statesville with a terrific story to tell. They had been out near Bostian Bridge when they all heard the horrific squeal of metal squeezing against metal, a loud crash that they swore sent the earth shaking beneath their feet and then a silence that gave way to anguished cries. They ran to the tracks but instead of finding a smoking wreck of a train, they saw something entirely unexpected.

A solitary figure stood on the tracks, gazing up at the sun. Using one hand as a makeshift visor, the figure peered up into the sky. In his other hand, he held a small gold watch that winked like a shimmering star in the bright sunlight. The figure frowned, took off his cap, wiped his brow and turned to the gawking bystanders. "Excuse me," the man said, "but would you please be kind enough to tell me the time?" He nodded toward his pocket watch. "It needs resetting." The bystanders looked at each other in disbelief; perhaps the strange man was in shock. They brushed past him and onto the bridge. Peering down, they saw nothing. There was no wrecked train. They turned back to the strange man and noticed that he was dressed in a baggage master's uniform. The man smiled at them, doffed his cap with a wink and then began walking down the tracks. He promptly faded from view. The people were stunned. Who had they just seen? Could that have been real? Some of them whispered that it just couldn't be. The man, after all, bore more than a passing resemblance to H.K. Linster, the baggage man who had perished a year ago in the great Bostian Bridge derailment. One man, as an afterthought, looked at his own pocket watch. It was three in the afternoon, the exact time that the train had derailed.

From that time on, it's been said in Statesville, North Carolina, that H.K. Linster will appear on the tracks of Bostian Bridge each year at the same time, upon the very same day that he plummeted to his untimely death so many years ago.

3
Spirits of the Past

The Bath Hoofprints

Bath, North Carolina has a storied and colorful history. For a short time in the early 18th century it was home to Edward Teach, better known as the dreaded pirate Blackbeard. In 1711, Tuscarora warriors attacked settlers along the Pamlico River, putting houses to the torch and slaughtering men, women and children. By the middle of the 18th century, Bath had recovered from the massacre and, blessed with a natural harbor and fertile soils, the little community was prospering. It very nearly became the capital of the state in 1746. Its citizens walked tall and proud. If you believe the folklore, though, it all came to an end when Reverend George Whitfield, a Methodist revivalist of the Great Awakening, visited Bath and, horrified by the carousing and merriment of its population, laid a curse on the town. He proclaimed that Bath would never prosper and would forever remain a village. A devastating hurricane in 1769 nearly destroyed the town, and a yellow fever epidemic decimated its population. Whitfield's curse, it seemed, had worked. Modern Bath rests almost entirely within the boundaries city planner John Lawson first laid out in the late 17th century.

Of course, little regard is given these days to curses and hexes. Bath, one of North Carolina's first communities, seems a quaint and serene place, steeped in history and lore. It is a living museum of sorts, home to some of the state's oldest homes as well as St. Thomas Church, the oldest church building still in use in all of North Carolina. The waters of both Bath Creek and Pamlico River, glistening veins of blue and white, shimmer nearby. With such natural beauty it's no wonder that Bath is a community of leisurely and relaxed rhythms that pays little mind to the Reverend George Whitfield of long ago. But mention the baffling case of the mysterious Bath Hoofprints and talk of a Bath curse doesn't seem so crazy after all.

In the early days of the 19th century, one of the more popular amusements for the young heady men of Bath was the Sunday horse races. Of all the racers, no one aroused more respect and fear than Jesse Elliot. Hard drinking, reckless and possessed of a mouth dirtier than any saloon spittoon, Elliot seemed blessed with a natural ability to ride horses. No matter what anyone thought of the man, when he was astride his horse Fury, Elliot was a vision of grace, pure and sublime. For as long as anyone could remember, Elliot had won the Sunday races and the bitterest among the defeated muttered darkly that he must have made a deal with the devil.

As Elliot's legend grew, so too did his boldness. He offered $100, a princely sum, to anyone who could best him. Riders from far and wide came to accept this challenge but each one walked away defeated, his shoulders slumped and his spirits sapped. Elliot followed each victory with long nights of carousing in local taverns and, convinced of his own invincibility, grew increasingly reckless and loathsome.

On Sunday, October 13, 1813, a stranger dressed in black rode into Bath. His horse was as dark as pitch, with blood-red eyes that could have been plucked from the devil himself and large sinewy muscles that rippled beneath his hide. The rider approached Elliot and, in a hoarse whisper, demanded a race. For a moment, even the normally unflappable Elliot balked. But then he recovered himself and told the stranger, "Be at the track in one hour."

Elliot returned home to prepare. He downed two generous shots of his home-brewed liquor, a concoction so vile and fierce it was said that it could strip the green from the forest. Before he left, his wife came to him and pleaded with him not to race anymore. A God-fearing woman, she had long protested against Elliot racing on Sundays and begged him once more to walk the path of righteousness. Elliot, vain, proud and wrathful, scoffed at his wife, dismissing her with the back of his hand. As he rode away, his wife called out after him, "You'll be sent straight to hell this day."

Elliot rode to the track, where he saw the dark stranger waiting. Elliot hesitated once more; he felt pinpricks of uncertainty in his stomach and for a moment thought that just maybe he should listen to his wife. Then he heard the roar of the crowd, saw the long wave of fists raised in his support and felt his confidence return. Elliot guided Fury next to the dark rider.

In a flash, the riders were off. The earth shook beneath the thundering hooves, and the gathered crowd watched with wide-mouthed surprise as the dark rider stormed to the lead.

Elliot spurred his horse on, and spectators recalled how he yelled out, "Take me in a winner or take me to hell!" Elliot's horse surged forth to the increasing applause of the rapt audience and, with each stride, Fury closed the gap. The crowd lustily roared its approval. "Get 'im, Elliot!" they cried. "Come on, Fury!" But as the horses approached the first turn of the dirt track, Fury suddenly twisted his head, shied away from the turn and planted his hooves firmly into the ground. Elliot was launched violently from his saddle, his body flying through the air like a human arrow. With a gasp-inducing thud, Elliot crashed headfirst into the thick trunk of a pine

The town of Bath has a storied and colorful history.

tree. His body dropped gracelessly to the ground. Hair from his head hung from the bark of the tree, which was now speckled with grotesque splashes of blood and fragments of bone and teeth. Silence fell upon the track like a shroud. The dark rider vanished, his tracks ending abruptly in the middle of the track.

"He was the devil himself," locals proclaimed. "The rider came and took Elliot straight to hell with him!" News of Elliot's bizarre demise made its rounds in the homes, taverns, churches and streets of Bath. Neighbors living near the track spread the word that the side of the tree against which Elliot's brains had been dashed had turned brown and died while the other half remained lush and green. Surely here was proof of the deal Elliot had made with the devil. As further evidence, villagers pointed to the soil. Days, weeks and even months after the accident, Fury's hoofprints were still as fresh and clear as the day they had been made.

The townspeople of Bath interpreted the hoofprints as a sign from God. Surely God had been displeased with the disrespect of the Sabbath and left the hoofprints as a reminder of the tragic fate young sinners would suffer. "Repent now or suffer a trip to hell like Jesse Elliot!" became the mantra of local pastors. Their advice was heeded. Local belief holds that as word of Elliot's frightening death spread, respect of the Sabbath grew significantly in and around Bath. As the years passed, the story was handed down from one generation to the next, as sure and steady as the hoofprints themselves.

Reportedly, Fury's hoofprints are still visible, even today. They seem possessed of mystical qualities, resisting decay and erosion. Though the hoofprints are exposed to the elements, they remain shockingly free of grass, weeds, pine needles or any other sort of detritus. Children have grown up enacting a ritual over a century old. On their way to school, they fill the depressions with whatever dirt, paper bags or crumpled notebook pages are available; no matter what they deposit in them, the depressions always end up free of debris. Sometimes all it takes is a few hours. But it could be longer, say a day or a week. Regardless, the depressions always end up free of debris.

In the 1950s, word of the Bath phenomenon reached Earl Harrell, a newsreel cameraman. Intrigued, he traveled to Bath to see the infamous hoofprints for himself. As he wandered the village inquiring about the hoofprints, locals told him about an experiment he could try for himself. They directed Harrell to scatter corn all over the site and promised that chickens would eat up every last kernel, save for the ones that had fallen into the hoofprints. Harrell was incredulous but curious. He set up his camera, scattered the corn and waited. Darned if the Bath residents weren't right. Harrell watched, fascinated, as chickens hungrily picked the ground clean of feed everywhere except in the depressions.

Harrell devised an experiment of his own, just in case he was the unfortunate victim of a local prank or hoax. He filled the depressions with pine needles, leaves, dirt and pebbles and then laid a web of fine black netting over the prints. In the morning, to Harrell's utter amazement and disbelief, the impressions were empty, though Harrell's netting remained intact. Science has yet to come up with a theory solid enough to explain the seeming immutability of the hoofprints, and it is certainly one of the most intriguing phenomena, not just of North Carolina, but of the world.

The Bath Hoofprints, situated about a mile outside of the community, are still plainly visible, though catching a glimpse of them is a difficult task. They're on private land and the property owners, by all accounts, do not take kindly to trespassers. One needn't worry, though. The hoofprints have been there since the early 19th century. It's a good bet that they'll be around for a long time to come.

Hannah's Creek Swamp

During the Civil War, military rules usually forbade plundering. Of course, there were exceptions, notably during Sherman's March to the Sea and the Carolinas Campaign. The men who were allowed to plunder were called bummers and were given rigid restrictions. They were not to use threatening or abusive language, could not enter private homes and were expected to leave enough food and supplies for families to survive. However, many of these bummers, disillusioned and disheartened by the war and the harsh conditions it bred, saw an opportunity to line their pockets and gain something tangible for their sacrifice. They became despicable marauders who answered to no authority and who murdered innocent civilians then pillaged their homes. Having seen their companions slaughtered like animals on the battlefields, these men became beasts themselves.

According to local legend, one such band of marauders, led by David Fanning, wreaked havoc throughout the South, following the smoking trail of destruction Sherman and his men had blazed toward the end of the Civil War. Sherman had followed through on his promise to "make Georgia howl," but it was Fanning and others of his ilk who made the state bleed. Fanning ransacked homes, claiming their valuables and supplies as his own. His was a merciless touch; had he displayed the slightest bit of compassion, he might very well have lived to see the end of the war as a Confederate prisoner of war. As it was, when he murdered Confederate Colonel John Saunders and his wife at their home near Smithfield, he set in motion a chain of events that would lead not just to his death, but also to the death of 50 of his men.

The late Colonel John Saunders had a son, Confederate Lieutenant John Saunders, who vowed revenge for his father's death. He requisitioned his general for a troop of men to help him clear Johnston County of the roving bands of merciless marauders. The weeks passed as Saunders relentlessly pursued these renegades, but he still found himself no closer to catching his parents' killers. He began to despair until he received word that a band of Union men had been seen taking refuge on a tiny island amidst the waters of Hannah's Creek Swamp. It was a good lead—the best, in fact, that he had heard in days.

When Saunders arrived at Hannah's Creek Swamp, he realized that his men could hardly expect to gain access to the island unnoticed. The element of surprise was critical, and Saunders meant not to squander it. He and his men dressed themselves in clothing borrowed from Smithfield locals, who were more than willing to help. Thus disguised, they rowed to the island. When asked to identify himself and his men, Saunders said that they were Yankees fleeing from a neighboring county and seeking refuge.

Fanning and his men never suspected a thing until Saunders stepped off his boat, at which point they became aware that they had been trapped. With the guns of Saunders' men trained on them, Fanning and his marauders surrendered quietly. The men were searched and stripped of their ill-gotten goods. Saunders himself searched Fanning, and when he came across a necklace adorned with a crucifix of gold, he knew that his quest had come to an end. The necklace had been his mother's. A terrible rage filled Saunders.

He ordered all of Fanning's men hanged. As the bodies of his 50 men twisted and turned from the gnarled branches of his island refuge, Fanning recoiled in horror, compelled to watch by the gun at the back of his head. Fanning begged for his life, but Saunders had other plans.

Fanning was tied up and carried back to the boats, his pleas for mercy ignored. Saunders escorted Fanning back to the Saunders' home and into the family graveyard. Two new headstones adorned the little cemetery, and Fanning was hanged above these markers.

The Civil War may have ended in 1864, but its echoes still reverberate throughout the land. One area where they resound the most is in Hannah's Creek Swamp. It's there that Fanning's marauders have been seen swinging from the trees, a century and a half after their ragged bodies were picked clean by scavengers. Witnesses have often been startled by eerie pleas for mercy emanating from somewhere deep within the swamp. Many people believe the pleader is the ghost of David Fanning, still begging for mercy though he, as a marauder, had shown none.

Although there have been plenty of sightings, skeptics like to point out that very little of the account can be verified. Did Fanning and his men actually exist? If so, then where exactly was their island hideout? No one knows. Some say that it's near Devil's Racetrack, though people who have searched there claim that all you'll find is a small, shallow swamp that is getting smaller and shallower. Still, the skeptics have done little to deter ghost hunters or enthusiasts such as Ted Bucklin (name changed).

Bucklin lived in nearby Smithfield for a couple of years in the early 1990s, and during that time, he made a few treks down Highway 701 to Hannah's Creek Swamp. "It's real swampy, all right," Bucklin says. "I never did find an island and, well, there's not really any place I'd imagine you'd want to hide. But it's been a long time since the Civil War. Things change. Maybe the swamp has too." Bucklin, in fact, never expected to find an island; he only hoped to catch a glimpse of the supernatural. And he claims he did.

"Now, I never saw any bodies swinging in the air or anything," he says, "but I definitely heard and felt something." Bucklin traveled there on a relatively warm autumn night. The air was thick, humid and teeming with mosquitoes whose low, incessant whine provided an eerie soundtrack.

"I was just wandering along," he says, "and I hadn't been wandering long before I heard something really bizarre." It sounded like someone was breathing heavily, as if exhausted. At first Bucklin thought that maybe someone was hurt and needed help, but when he called out and ventured into the swamp, no one answered. He was alone. "The breathing continued," he says, "and then, in this really weak voice, I heard somebody say, 'Spare me.'" It continued, over and over, like some haunting refrain, before the voice, as if summoning the last of its strength, bellowed out, "Please!" Then there was silence. Bucklin remembers standing there, in the heat and humidity, and suddenly feeling very cold.

"It was like I'd suddenly stepped into a walk-in freezer," Bucklin marvels. "I was freezing. And shivering. If I walked a couple of feet in either direction, I warmed right up. But make no mistake, there was some sort of cold spot there and it gave me the creeps." Bucklin didn't stay long. Spooked, he beat a hasty retreat to his car and drove back to Smithfield as quickly as he could. He just had to get out of there. "I never did go back," he recalls. "There was this part of me that really wanted to, but I just didn't. After hearing the stories about those marauders, I didn't really want to see bodies hanging from trees. That voice was enough."

Bucklin had perhaps heard the voice of David Fanning, still paying penance many years later for his woeful crimes. Given his dark deeds, it seems a just and measured punishment.

Mill Creek Swamp

Not too far from Hannah's Creek Swamp, an old bridge crosses Mill Creek. Here, strange and spooky things have allegedly been happening for over a century. It's a fascinating mystery with its roots in a murder that took place long ago.

In 1820, the land around the Mill Creek Bridge was owned by a slave owner known simply (and ominously) as Lynch. By all accounts, Lynch was particularly cruel and vicious. He worked his slaves ceaselessly; if their spirits and strength should flag, he never hesitated to lash them with his ever-ready whip. Lynch was a humorless man, and it was said that the only things that ever brought a smile to his creased and weathered face were the sound of his whip striking the flesh of his slaves and the inevitable groans and whimpers that followed.

Not surprisingly, he was reviled, and his slaves often looked longingly to the west, quietly urging the sun to fall beneath the horizon so their days would come to an end. Many wondered what it would be like to strike and kill Lynch, to repay him in kind for the scars that lined their backs and limbs, but it was only fanciful thinking. Who'd defend them if they did? Instead, they chose stoicism, suffering Lynch's daily abuse in silence. Lynch apparently believed that he had broken the collective spirits of his slaves, and the belief only served to hone his cruelty. He was wrong, having grossly underestimated the perseverance and strength of the human spirit.

One day, Lynch ordered a hand named Old Squire to clear land around the Mill Creek Bridge. It was exhausting work, and Old Squire, whose strength had ebbed with age, found it nearly impossible to keep up the pace that his master had set. Lynch was furious and let Old Squire know it. Throughout the long day, he lashed Old Squire repeatedly and with growing fury. Old Squire felt a rage surging through his body and did his best to suppress it. With the sun hanging low over the horizon and lengthening shadows creeping across the land, Old Squire knew that rest and relief were soon to come. Lynch, however, had other plans in mind.

Even in the gloom of twilight, Lynch, lantern in hand, continued to work Old Squire. The whip arced through the air repeatedly. Eventually, Lynch whipped Old Squire one too many times. Something snapped, like dry kindling, in Old Squire's mind. He turned toward Lynch and, with his remaining strength, swung his rusty, jagged hoe at his stunned master. He struck Lynch in the head, fairly cleaving it into two. Lynch's twitching body fell from his horse, and his lantern tumbled to the ground with a dull thud. The spooked horse whinnied and fled. Old Squire was horrified. Lynch was dead. Moving quickly, Old Squire took up his hoe once more and dug a shallow grave. Satisfied, he dragged Lynch's body into the pit and buried him.

Old Squire returned to the slave quarters and didn't utter a word about what had happened. When people began to wonder the next day where Lynch had gone, Old Squire stayed quiet then, too. Lynch's family, fearful for Lynch's life since his horse had returned riderless the night before, sent their slaves out into the fields and the countryside to look for him. Old Squire, for his part, volunteered to search around the Mill Creek Bridge, hoping to keep the body hidden.

Despite Old Squire's silence and craft, people began wondering exactly what had happened at the Mill Creek Bridge.
Not long after Lynch's disappearance, bizarre and eerie
things began occurring around the site. Riders reported that
while they crossed the bridge, their torches would mysteriously extinguish themselves only to re-ignite once they were
on the other side. Some horses refused to cross the span,
rearing up in terror as they approached. Other witnesses
reported hearing the crack of a whip near the bridge and seeing a small ball of light hovering above it.

In perhaps the most bizarre account, an old man crossing
the bridge had his cane wrested from him by an unseen
force. Undaunted, he soldiered on, picking his way gingerly
across the bridge. When he reached the other side, he
received a most peculiar surprise. There, lying among the
blades of grass, was his cane.

Lynch's disappearance remained unsolved until Old
Squire's death. With his last few breaths, Old Squire, perhaps
wanting to clear the slate before he entered the afterlife,
finally recounted what he had done to Lynch and where he
had buried the body. Not long after, Old Squire passed away.
The morning after his death, men armed with shovels and
hoes ventured out to Mill Creek Bridge to recover Lynch's
body. They needn't have bothered with the tools. His corpse
was found lying on the bridge. The ground beneath was
undisturbed, and, by all appearances, it seemed that Lynch's
body had somehow found a way to transport itself from its
grave beneath the bridge to the wooden walkway above.
Nobody ever did determine how Lynch's body was unearthed.

Years later, the story of Old Squire and Lynch still arouses
curiosity, though it seems that time has sapped the energy of

the spirits. Modern-day accounts of the Mill Creek Bridge are relatively tame compared to its spectacular lore. These days, only the ball of light is seen on the bridge as Lynch and Old Squire, their afterlives tied together in a way neither of them could have imagined, continue to clear the land.

Historic Stagville

Seven miles north of Durham, near Treyburn, sprawls the remains of what once was the largest plantation of the ante-bellum South. Its owners were the Bennehan-Cameron Family and by 1860, they had acquired almost 30,000 acres and, to maintain it all, a virtual army of 900 slaves. Settlement of the area had begun in the 18th century and by the turn of the 19th century, Virginian Richard Bennehan had amassed close to 4000 acres and 40 slaves. He grew tobacco and grain and raised livestock, and through judicious marriages, notably with the Cameron family, his holdings were vastly increased. In 1954, Liggett and Myers, a tobacco company, acquired the property and in 1976 deeded 71 acres to the state of North Carolina.

Today, Historic Stagville is a national historic landmark and serves as a learning site dedicated to educating the public about the slave communities upon which the plantation prospered. Two-story slave quarters, erected by the slaves themselves—few of whom had any formal carpentry training—still stand as silent testaments to the darkest shame of American history. Unlike many slave dwellings that fell quickly into ruin after emancipation, five former Stagville slave houses at Horton Grove, many in their original condition, were maintained by the African American residents. Still standing as well are the Bennehan House, constructed in 1787, and the Great Barn, erected in 1860. Walking through Historic Stagville feels as if you've been thrust backwards in time to the early 19th century, to a far different world. What's most striking is the remarkable development of the slave community, which—despite forced illiteracy and the slave owner's imposition of inferiority—was able to form its own distinct culture. That it still speaks to visitors today testifies to the perseverance of the human spirit. Recovered artifacts speak volumes, but at Historic Stagville, the past is also resurrected through the presence of the spirits haunting its grounds.

Patty Foster still clearly remembers the field trip she and her classmates took to Historic Stagville in the late 1990s. From Durham herself, Patty had long been fascinated with the Civil War. She had collected dozens of accounts of haunted battlefields, homes and sites. She could barely contain her excitement as she climbed up the steps into the yellow school bus. As other students strolled around the Bennehan House, boredom etched clearly into their faces, Patty excitedly took it all in. The house had been restored and when she closed her eyes, she felt almost as if she were back in the antebellum South. As she approached the staircase, Patty remembers feeling something unusual. "It was strange," she recalls, her honeyed North Carolina accent growing with her excitement, "I suddenly got the distinct feeling that we were all being watched, that there was someone or something else in the room with us."

In one room, which had served as a nursery, squatted a cradle and a rocking chair. Patty entered and stared, fascinated, as the cradle and rocking chair slowly began swaying back and forth, as if a Bennehan matriarch were sitting in the chair, rocking her cradled babe to sleep. Patty shook her head, thinking that it had been a draft, but when she looked at the window, it was tightly shut. "They were definitely moving," she says, "moved by an unseen force." Excitedly, Patty hurried back down the stairs to join her fellow students, who had begun walking down the long dirt road leading to the slave quarters.

When they reached the two-story dwellings, the strange feeling Patty had felt on the staircase returned. With chills running up and down the length of her spine, Patty began walking around the quarters. "Suddenly, I got the feeling as if someone was standing right behind me, as if somebody was boring holes into my back," she recalls. Slowly and tremulously, Patty turned around and saw, standing before her, a young black girl. "She looked so real," Patty says, "and I thought she was." The girl looked distraught; tears had caked the dirt that dusted her face like a fine powder. Patty approached the girl gingerly, bent down to offer a comforting hand, only to watch in amazement as the small child turned, walked away and faded into the air, like your breath on a cold winter day.

Patty rubbed her eyes. The girl had definitely vanished. Had she imagined it all? Had it all been just a hallucination? Only later, when she mentioned the girl to Historic Stagville tour guides, did she learn that she was not the only one to have seen the girl. Many people had over the years, with some claiming that the apparition even spoke, asking balefully if anyone had seen her deceased father. With a smile, Patty learned that she had been far more courageous in approaching the girl than even some of Historic Stagville's staff. Grounds people had often dropped their equipment and fled Horton Grove as quickly as they could after encountering the little girl. Patty left that day feeling relieved and sad that she couldn't spend more time exploring the grounds. After all, the tour guide had told her that the little girl isn't the only spirit of Historic Stagville.

Patty stared as the rocking chair swayed slowly back and forth.

Walter Shank had been looking for something different to do for Halloween. He was too old for trick or treating and was tired of wearing costumes. So, in 2004, when he learned that Historic Stagville was offering a ghost tour, he figured he'd check it out. Storytellers had been placed around the site, each offering varied accounts of the Stagville ghosts. The most memorable for Walter was the storyteller at Horton Grove, a man named Lane who was an expert on Historic Stagville. Lane had grown up right next to the site and had spent many an afternoon playing around the old slave quarters. One evening, he was in Horton Grove when dusk fairly turned to day. Everything around him was suddenly cast in a reddish glow that almost made it seem as if the land itself were on fire. He turned to see that from within one of the slave houses, a red fiery glow burned, illuminating all the windows. Terrified, Lane ran home. When he reached his house, he turned, only to see that the building was now dark and still. His parents were incensed and angrily demanded to know what little Lane had been doing playing with matches at the old slave houses. Over the years, more than one fire engine has been called to Historic Stagville to put out a reported fire only to find the building, whether it is a slave quarter or the Great Barn, intact and decidedly not on fire. A number of firemen have reported seeing what they claim to be the apparition of a black slave watching from the loft.

Lane had riveted Walter, but still, the latter was a little skeptical. "I'd never really believed in ghosts," Walter says. "But this guy certainly got me thinking." And as Walter continued around Historic Stagville, he couldn't help but feel as if everything were a little different. A sense of expectation hung in the air. When he reached the Great Barn, he, along with a number of other individuals, heard what sounded like footsteps coming from the barn's now non-existent third floor. And throughout the evening, Walter swore that he saw "balls of light just floating all over the site... I read that they're supposed to be the energies of moving ghosts." Walter left, a little shaken. "I won't lie to you," he says. "I was definitely, well, spooked. And there's definitely something unusual about that place."

Later that same night, Historic Stagville staffers were closing up the Benehan House. Motion detectors had been set and the doors and windows locked. As they turned to leave, something inside the house caught their attention. Bouncing by the window was a small light, as if someone inside was walking the floor with a candle in his or her hand. The staffers looked at each other, making sure that they were all indeed out of the building. They were.

Historic Stagville staffers have had many encounters with the plantation's restless spirits. The spirits are mischievous in nature, fond of locking and unlocking doors in front of the eyes of disbelieving staffers, murmuring sweet nothings and pacing around the creaking floorboards. According to *Haunted North Carolina*, one evening, a staff member was locking the Benehan House when the sound of footsteps from the second floor caught her attention. With a frown, she opened the door and walked up the stairs. After a careful search of all the rooms, she saw that she was alone. Quickly and a little more nervously now, she set the alarm again and locked the door. From a safe distance, she watched the building for a while, determined to see if anyone would emerge from its shadows. No one did. The staff member, with her patience at an end, finally left.

When she returned the next morning, she immediately asked her supervisor if anything strange had happened during the evening. The supervisor looked at her crookedly and then nodded. The motion detector had been tripped, though oddly enough, not the alarm system itself. And then the supervisor brandished a skeleton key. The staff member recognized it immediately. It usually rested in the keyhole of the front door and she distinctly remembered leaving it there. The supervisor revealed that the key had been found lying on an antique couch, several feet away from the front door.

With so many accounts, it's to be expected that Historic Stagville has become popular with local paranormal investigators. In May 2004, Haunted North Carolina's investigators, Jim Hall, David Gurney and Waverly Hawthorne, examined the location. As they worked in the Great Barn, Waverly, who was exploring the stalls, experienced a succession of sudden headaches in various spots and saw what looked like a shadow move through his line of sight. Photographs taken in the barn came out blurred. At Horton Grove, Gurney told Hall that someone was watching them, and that it was most likely a young, African-American girl. Bear in mind that at the time, Gurney had no knowledge of the spirit who had frightened groundskeepers. Only later did the team learn from a staff member of the young spirit.

In October 2004, Paranormal Research of Occurances (sic) Beyond Explanation, or as it's better known, PROBE, sent an investigative team of their own to Historic Stagville. Haunted North Carolina was there as well, working at the visitor's center. While PROBE's team experienced nothing unusual, tour guides and other tour groups did report bizarre and unexplainable activity. It seems that, without a doubt, Historic Stagville is haunted. It's not a surprise, given its past. Historic Stagville, which aims to preserve the past so that people may learn from it, appears to have achieved its goals.

Fort Fisher

Known as the "Gibraltar of the Confederacy," Fort Fisher today is little but sand and oak. In its time, it was perhaps the greatest and most impregnable of Confederate forts during the Civil War. It was the last major stronghold of the Confederacy until it fell in the waning months of the conflict. By 1865, Fort Fisher stood in defense of the only supply line left open to blockade runners and Confederate General Robert E. Lee's Army of Northern Virginia. If it were severed, the Confederacy would surely fall. On January 15, 1865, the Union launched a massive amphibious assault on the fort. It finally fell and contributed greatly to the Confederacy's eventual defeat.

At the beginning of the Civil War, the Confederacy assumed control of a peninsula in southern North Carolina near the mouth of the Cape Fear River. Construction began on an earthwork fortification to defend the all-important port of Wilmington. Its planners took inspiration from Malakoff Tower (a Crimean War fort) in Sebastopol, Russia, and it came to occupy a mile of sea defense and a third of a mile of land defense. It was constructed largely of earth and sand, the better to absorb the blows of heavy explosives. Twenty-two guns faced the sea while twenty-five faced land. These cannons pounded Union blockading ships, keeping them at bay and providing a safe haven for both Wilmington and Confederate ships.

Union war planners understood the fort's importance and finally launched an assault upon its walls on Christmas Eve 1864. For two days, Federal infantry threw themselves against the fort, only to be repelled as Union warships pounded the fort from the sea. Little progress, if any, was made. Realizing that Fort Fisher was too strong for their assault, Union commanders retreated in a humiliating defeat. Plans were immediately made for a second assault. Gustavus Fox, Assistant Secretary of the Navy, pressed urgently for success. "The country will not forgive us for another failure at Wilmington," he said gravely.

In late December, Union soldiers under the command of Major General Alfred Terry were on the move toward Fort Fisher. On the morning of January 12, 1865, an armada of 58 warships set sail under the command of Admiral David Porter and by evening, Fort Fisher's planner and commander, Colonel William Lamb, bore witness to an awesome sight. "I saw from the ramparts of the fort the lights of the great armada," he later said, "as one after another appeared on the horizon." It was a formidable armada and among the ships were transports carrying 8500 men. The following day, ironclads and gunboats began their bombardment of the fort in an assault Lamb called "beyond description."

Union troops began landing four miles north of the fort completely uncontested, just miles removed from Department of Wilmington commander General Braxton Bragg, his men, several artillery batteries and 1500 North Carolina Reserves who had dug in at Sugar Loaf. Fearful of weakening their own lines, they simply allowed Federal troops to land, to the great consternation and frustration of Confederate General William Whiting.

Bragg had commended both Whiting and Lamb for their defense of Fort Fisher in December, but while Bragg staged reviews of his troops, Whiting and Lamb petitioned for more guns, men and ammunition. Bragg ignored them. And now, as shells pounded Fort Fisher and Confederate ammunition ran low, he refused to send aid while Lamb ordered his batteries to fire only once every half hour. Whiting was incensed. He demanded that Bragg reinforce the fort, and then sailed alone down the river to Fort Fisher. Entering the fort, he approached Lamb and said, "Lamb, my boy, I have come to share your fate. You and your garrison are to be sacrificed." Lamb was devastated, left in utter disbelief that Bragg had essentially deserted the fort.

In the early hours of January 14, 1865, Union troops advanced upon the fort and were hard at work constructing a line of entrenchments spanning the entire width of the peninsula. Bragg did probe the line tentatively from the north, but quickly withdrew after determining that the Union position was too strong for an assault. Whiting grew incandescent with rage. He knew all too well what the Union had in store but could only watch, helpless. He cabled Bragg with a message. "The game of the enemy is very plain," he said. "The enemy has extended to the riverbank. This they should never have been allowed to do…if they are permitted to remain there the reduction of Fort Fisher is but a question of time…I will hold this place to the last extremities, but unless you drive that land force from its position, I cannot answer for the security of this harbor."

Bragg, finally spurred to action, dispatched a portion of General Robert Hoke's division with the spurious boast that these men would render the fort "impregnable against assault." He was wrong. By nightfall, most of the guns lining Fort Fisher's northern battlements had been pounded into dust. Union commanders planned their infantry assault.

Hoke's division arrived the following morning but it was hardly enough. As Whiting watched the sea of blue-uniformed Federal soldiers rippling across the peninsula, he urgently cabled Bragg again. "The enemy are about to assault; they outnumber us heavily," he wrote. "Nearly all land guns disabled. Attack! Attack! It is all I can say and all you can do." Bragg decided to send further reinforcements to Fort Fisher, dispatching 1000 men from Johnson Hagood's brigade. It was an inane gambit. The men had to pick their way northward from the southern end of the peninsula across two miles of land as enemy shells from the Union fleet exploded around them "like the roar of heavy peals of thunder." Only 350 men arrived at Fort Fisher, increasing the fort's garrison to just 1900 men. At 3:25 PM, the Union fleet stopped its bombardment and together they emitted an ear-splitting blast from their steam whistles, a fitting accompaniment to what Lieutenant Commander William B. Cushing of the USS *Monticello* would later call "the death dance of the hundreds about to fall."

Fleet Captain K. R. Breese impulsively launched the attack with his naval shore contingent without waiting to coordinate with Union infantry forces, and he sent his men screaming and charging toward the fort below the Northeast Bastion. Whiting and Lamb stalked the fort's ramparts, exhorting their men and urging them to defend the fort. With just revolvers and cutlasses, Breese's marines fell like stalks of wheat before the scythe, cut down where they stood by a rain of murderous fire. They retreated quickly. Lamb, Whiting and their men cheered loudly. They had repulsed the attack. But the cheers faded fast. They turned to see several large Union flags waving over the western portion of the fort and a flood of several thousand Federal soldiers pouring through gaps opened up in the fortifications—a rushing tide of men surely sent by the Angel of Death himself.

The Federal troops advanced and Fort Fisher began to fall. At 6:30 PM, Whiting sent one final plea to Bragg at Sugar Loaf: "The enemy are assaulting us by land and sea. Their infantry outnumber us. Can't you help us? I am slightly wounded." Unbelievably, as Confederate resistance at Fort Fisher teetered, Bragg cabled authorities in Wilmington, assuring them that everything at the fort was under control. At ten o'clock in the evening, just two hours after Bragg assured Wilmington that Fort Fisher would not fall, rockets and fireworks filled the night sky above the fort as Union forces celebrated their victory. President of the Confederacy Jefferson Davis was stunned. "The intelligence is sad as it was unexpected," he said. The Gibraltar of the Confederacy had fallen. A short time later, Confederate forts throughout the area were abandoned. Wilmington fell under Union control as well, and within months, Lee surrendered at Appomattox.

Bragg informed Confederate General Lee of Fort Fisher's loss: "I am mortified at having to report the unexpected capture of Fort Fisher, with most of its garrison." Five hundred Confederate men had been slain and many more taken prisoner. Among those taken prisoner that day was General William B. Whiting, who, although grievously wounded, was taken to the Union prison stockade on Governor's Island in New York Harbor. On March 10, 1865, he died from wounds sustained in his valiant defense of Fort Fisher. He had been one of the best generals of the Confederacy. At West Point, the man from Mississippi had graduated at the top of his class and had ably commanded a division with Lee's mighty

Army of Northern Virginia. Having given himself over so fully—emotionally and physically—to the Confederate cause at Fort Fisher, it's not surprising that his ghost is said to roam the grounds.

Today, very little of what was once the fearsome Fort Fisher remains. A palisade fence has been restored along with 10 percent of the fortifications. It is a national historic landmark, blessed with a pristine shoreline of gleaming white sandy beaches. Its bucolic splendor hardly hints at the horrors it has witnessed or the blood that once stained the earth. It's said that Whiting returns to walk the parapets across which he once raged as Federal marines tried to storm the fort. He's caught the attention of more than one visitor to the site.

Jesse Pipkin and his daughter Fran journeyed to Fort Fisher not long ago. After the tour had ended, they began walking the beach. Fran played delightedly in the sand, digging through it with her hands in hopes of maybe finding a sea star, or even better, an urchin. Jesse kept one eye on his child, the other on the gulls and terns that soared through the air and danced above the waves of the Atlantic. He turned his head and saw, walking toward the fort, what he describes as "a group of figures, marching in lockstep and in formation." Even though they were crossing the sand, they glided across it, "as if their feet didn't sink into the stuff." The men were garbed in the dark blue uniforms of the Union and they came closer and closer. Jesse saw his daughter playing in the surf and called out to her. "Get back here," he yelled. She sat directly in the soldiers' path. She didn't seem to hear him so Jesse ran toward her. With the soldiers just yards away, he scooped Fran up in his arms, threw a quick glance at the spirits and ran toward his car. "I'll never forget what I saw," he says. "Those ghosts or things—they had no limbs, no face. They were just uniforms gliding across the sand." Looking up at the fort, Jesse could swear that he saw a lone figure standing above the fort, as if scanning the beach for signs of approaching Federal troops. Jesse and Fran drove away from the fort as quickly as possible. When he began conducting research into the fort, Jesse soon learned that he was not alone in what he had seen. Stories about the ghosts of Fort Fisher rise up thick and fast and he quickly determined that the lone figure could only have been General William Whiting.

There are other ghosts besides Whiting at Fort Fisher. One, whose name is forever lost, is known simply as The Sentinel: a ghostly Confederate soldier who stands watch in the pine tree grove north of the fort. At the beginning of the 20th century, two men were out hunting ducks when they caught sight of what's been called a "watcher in the woods." The figure seemed composed completely of a gray spectral mist. It frightened the hunters into dropping their ducks and running away. Days later, one of their friends, who'd listened to their story with great interest and curiosity, decided to explore the pine tree grove. He found what he assumed to be the barrel of an old rifle, exactly the sort a Confederate sentinel might have used at his post.

More recently, John Goode, who had been a site manager at Bentonville, another haunted Civil War site, arrived at Fort Fisher for a living history event. Late one evening, he was walking in the woods north of the fort when the sound of a horse neighing and snorting near him startled him from his thoughts. He turned, scanning the darkness, but could see and hear nothing else. Despite his determined search, Goode found nothing but trees and shadow. He finally concluded that it must have been a fellow re-enactor on horseback, but later learned that no horses had been out on the grounds— anywhere—that evening.

Employees of Fort Fisher have often reported hearing doors slam and open even when locked and barred shut. Many of them have also seen the lone figure in gray, purported to be General William Whiting, wandering the grounds. With the high number of eyewitness accounts, it's not surprising that paranormal researchers have descended upon Fort Fisher to unlock its mysteries.

Members of Seven Paranormal Research, a group based in Carthage, North Carolina, arrived at the site, laden with cameras, video recorders, tape recorders and electromagnetic field sensors to see for themselves whether or not the site is truly haunted. Investigators arrived one sunny afternoon to map the location and then returned two weeks later for a nightlong investigation. They gathered a great deal of interesting data, to say the least.

Three separate investigators saw a man standing on a knoll a little after midnight. All felt the warmth drain from the air, and an infrared thermometer showed that the temperature had dropped sharply from 68 to 43 degrees. Motion detectors set around the knoll had not been tripped off and investigators were certain that it could have been nothing but a spirit. Separate of each other, the three investigators all stated that the figure was of "average height, lean and wearing gray with a hat pulled down over his forehead. He faced southeast and simply faded..." At the same time, other members of the investigative team were working opposite the knolls and had written in their notebooks, a little after midnight, that they experienced the strongest feeling of being watched.

Not long after, a pair of investigators heard what sounded like a cry for help coming from the beach. They set out with a dog in tow to explore but found nothing amiss. Oddly enough though, whenever they walked from a specific knoll past the oak grove, the dog would whine and growl. What was he growling at? The investigators couldn't say. In two locations the investigators discovered that they couldn't shake the sensation of being watched. "You could actually step into and out of this area and feel the change," the investigators wrote on their website.

In the 20-foot section, puzzled investigators who had done a thorough equipment check before that night suddenly found that their flashlights began to malfunction. Their cameras also jammed; film refused to advance and shutters failed to release. Most peculiarly of all, it seemed that something in the air was sucking the juice from their fresh batteries. Digital cameras, flashlights and camera flashes all died quickly, their batteries drained.

There is a bridge that spans the marshy land where countless Union soldiers were mowed down beneath artillery fire. On the eastern side of the bridge, investigators discovered that if they stood in a particular spot they were overwhelmed with sensations of cold and depression, and the most eerie sensation of something crushing their chests. One woman couldn't stand it; she burst into tears and left the bridge. Photographs taken at the location that night did not develop.

Developed photographs from other locations on the site yielded intriguing images including the shadowy figure of what may be General Whiting himself as well as The

Sentinel. EVP recordings picked up the sound of gunfire, while infrared video showed an orb floating across the screen to the beat of what sounds like marching footsteps. A tape recording captured the footsteps as well. The investigators determined that, without a doubt, Fort Fisher is haunted.

It was a conclusion also reached by Cape Fear Paranormal Investigations. Their pictures also recorded the appearance of a blurry, wraithlike figure and they also noted great drops in temperature, some as much as 15 degrees, and high EMF readings. All pointed to the presence of paranormal beings.

To be sure, Fort Fisher is a fascinating place. Its remains occupy what is today called Pleasure Island, a rather ironic name given the place's tortured and bloody past. It's a past that comes to life not just through the guided tours, but also through the presence of Union and Confederate soldiers, still mired in a battle that raged so many years ago.

The USS North Carolina

On October 27, 1937, work began in a New York naval ship-yard on a battleship the likes of which had never been seen. She was the first commissioned of the Navy's modern battle-ships and provoked such curiosity and attention that she quickly acquired the nickname "Showboat" throughout con-struction and fitting. Sponsored by Isabel Hoey, the daughter of North Carolina Governor Clyde R. Hoey, the ship was launched on June 13, 1940, and was commissioned at New York the following year on April 9. On June 10, 1942, the USS *North Carolina* entered the Pacific theater and served a role in every major Pacific engagement, notably Guadalcanal, Tarawa and Iwo Jima. She boasted a crew of 1880 men and formidable artillery, and she was crucial in the defense of air-craft carriers.

Before she was decommissioned in 1947, the USS *North Carolina* received 15 battle stars for service during World War II. By 1961, she was about to be sent to the scrap heap. Concerned North Carolinians began a campaign to "Save our Ship" and in September, the Navy transferred the *North Carolina* to the state that shared her name. On April 29, 1962, the USS *North Carolina* was dedicated at Wilmington as a memorial to the 10,000 North Carolinians who lost their lives in World War II.

Located on the opposite bank of the Cape Fear River across from downtown Wilmington, the USS *North Carolina* has become a popular tourist destination. Open year-round, the battleship still bears its 1944 camouflage. Most of its decks are open to visitors, though claustrophobics are advised that they may want to steer clear of the lower decks. Those with a fear of the paranormal might avoid the ship too, for although the existence of ghosts within the cramped confines of the USS *North Carolina* has not been conclusively proven, there is certainly enough anecdotal evidence to defy the skeptics.

For 27 years, Danny Bradshaw, a self-published writer who has recently published a book detailing the spirits of the USS *North Carolina,* worked on the decommissioned warship, often toiling long after the last tourist had gone home. Given his intimate working relationship with the ship, Bradshaw has become an expert on the spirits of the USS *North Carolina.* During its service in World War II, the USS *North Carolina* lost only 10 men, but that was enough to populate the halls of the ship with an assortment of ghosts. They are fond of appearing in doorways and behind portholes, opening and closing locked doors, turning television sets on and off and moving objects around rooms. Danny has heard mysterious voices coming from empty rooms and footsteps echoing through the ship, and has felt the requisite cold spots that usually accompany such phenomena. Though he has witnessed much of the bizarre activity for himself, hard evidence has been in short supply.

The spirits of the USS *North Carolina* may be restless, but even the spectral dead need a break every now and then. Long stretches of time have passed without a single paranormal incident, only to give way to a flurry of spirited activity. Intrigued by the possibilities, paranormal investigators descended upon the battleship in 2004 with the hopes of unlocking its secrets. Bradshaw welcomed their assistance. He advised the investigators to focus the bulk of their efforts on the battleship's port bow where, during a September 15, 1942 engagement, a Japanese torpedo struck and killed five members of the battleship's crew. In an interview with the Associated Press, Bradshaw said, "If there are any tortured souls onboard who might believe they died too young, it's probably these guys." Though Bradshaw admits that at times he's "felt a cold and evil feeling," for the most part, he believes that the spirits mean no one any harm.

The paranormal sleuths arrived during daylight and walked around the ship to familiarize themselves with the environment. Some pictures were taken and one, from the mess hall, revealed the presence of an orb. They left the ship for dinner and returned later in the evening to begin the bulk of their investigation. With EMF meters, infrared thermometers and motion detectors in tow, the investigators got down to work. Many of them frowned, noting that because of the ship's constant creaking and rolling, their audio and vibration monitors would be pretty much useless.

The investigators broke into three teams for the formal investigation. Following Bradshaw's advice, they set up three video cameras at three locations believed to be the most active. Rooms that they investigated included the engine room, Bradshaw's room, the sick bay and the mess hall. Not long after half past nine, one of the investigators noticed some movement in the chaplain's office. When the investigators returned to retrieve their video cameras, they were slightly irritated to discover that all their cameras had mysteriously shut themselves off. They pulled out the batteries, tested them and discovered that the batteries were still charged. The investigators attributed the electrical disruption to the spirits of the USS *North Carolina* and quickly determined that it was definitely alive with paranormal activity. The investigators' work is not yet complete. They have plans to return to the battleship to collect more information. For Bradshaw, the USS *North Carolina*'s night watchman, the results are encouraging, merely affirming what he's suspected for over 20 years.

The Little Red Man

Given Winston-Salem's long and storied history, it should surprise no one that scattered among the many tales of its past are those that are paranormal and supernatural in origin. Perhaps the most famous (or, depending on your point of view, infamous) account concerns the unfortunate and accidental death of a Moravian Brother named Andreas Kremser, better known these days as the Little Red Man.

In 1752, a band of mostly German settlers arrived in the wilds of North Carolina. They were all members of the *Unitas Fratrum*, or Moravian Church, an evangelical Christian communion first founded in the 15th century in Bohemia. Leading them was Bishop August Gottlieb Spangenberg. He bought close to 100,000 acres in Forsyth County and a year later, the first Moravian colony had been established in what would later be known as Salem (it merged in 1913 with Winston).

The day was March 25, 1786. Single Brother Andreas Kremser, a shoemaker and occasional gardener, sat quietly through the festal services, lost in his thoughts. With the evening services concluded, Brother Kremser returned to his room at the Single Brother House, the residence of Moravian bachelors, but he found sleep elusive. He was restless; his senses were alert and agitated. He decided to indulge in some work before going to sleep, and he headed to the dank, cold depths of the cellar that sprawled beneath the Single Brother House. A sweaty band of his Moravian brothers was there, excavating the earth for a planned addition.

With only feeble, flickering candlelight illuminating the depths, Brother Kremser picked up a shovel and joined the workers as they carved out a bank in the sandy soil. As their shadows danced across the walls and men took turns taking their well-earned rests, Kremser continued to dig. His breath came out in ragged pants and soon he found himself on his knees, the shovel's handle slippery beneath his sweaty palms. Still, there was something particularly restful about the toil and he dug farther, venturing deeper beneath the overhang they had created.

Many Brothers had argued against this method of excavation due to the particulate soil, but since it had proven successful in similar cases, their misgivings had been largely ignored. Only now did those who had cast aside the warnings realize how gravely foolhardy they had been to do so. As Brother Kremser continued to dig, with just his feet now peeking out from under the overhang, those around him realized with horror that the overhang was about to give way.

Urgently, they cried out to Brother Kremser but he couldn't hear their warnings. With a whisper that quickly turned into a roar, the overhang crumbled, pouring what seemed like tons of asphyxiating earth upon Kremser. Quickly, his Moravian Brothers set to digging him out. His left leg lay twisted at a horrible angle and his screams gave the most haunting hints of the pain that must surely have been wracking his body. Brother Lewis, a doctor, did what he could but, with a heavy heart, saw that a cure lay beyond what meager skills he possessed. Brother Kremser breathed his last breath a few hours later; his red coat, once brilliant and rich, was now dark and mottled. The tragedy was recorded within the Church Book of Salem Congregation as entry 45. But while Brother Kremser's physical being had expired, his spirit lingered.

From that day on, the laborers of Single Brother House often swore that another, unseen Moravian labored alongside them. Though they couldn't see Brother Kremser, they knew it was him. He had been a shoemaker, and the simple tap-tap-tap of his hammer had often been heard throughout the halls like the house's steady, rhythmic pulse. Even after his death, Brother Kresler continued to perfect his craft; his shoemaker's hammer carried on with its work. Every now and then, Brother Kresler would turn from his labors and the residents of Single Brother House would hear his footsteps rattling down the hall. In the basement, a buttressed cavern of twisting passageways, some saw the tail of his brilliant red coat flare from around a corner. "There goes Kremser," the brothers would say. The little man in red was also seen a number of times rushing past bedroom doorways.

In time, the Single Brother House, whose original purpose had been to house unmarried brothers, seemed less and less necessary, and finally it became a residence for families. Later still, the church converted it into a home for widows who spent their days wallowing in nostalgia and sharing the tales of their latest brushes with the house's little red man. One grandchild visiting her grandmother ran into the house one day, breathless and eyes wide with terror, to tell how her friend Betsy had seen a "little red man out there." The elderly women nodded in understanding, murmuring that they too had seen the little red man with a very friendly smile.

Playful and joyous, the little red man was never starved for company and seemed to take great delight in appearing and disappearing before the eyes of startled visitors. In one reported incident, two men were walking through the house's cellar. One of them was a visitor to Salem, unfamiliar with local lore, and as they walked, he heard the story of the Little Red Man. He scoffed at the stories, dismissing them as nothing but fairy tales. His guide agreed and the two chuckled loudly at the trusting nature and gullibility of their common man as they continued their walk through the cellar. No sooner had their laughter finished echoing through the cellar when, before their disbelieving eyes, a figure materialized. He was a small man clad in a bright red coat, and looking very much as if he had stepped from the guide's imagination and into reality. Amazed, the two men rushed the little red man, determined to capture him, but as they leapt at him, the little red man disappeared with a wink and a laugh, and the two men collapsed in a heap on the floor. They scrambled to their feet and, turning around, saw the specter grinning at them from the other end of the room. Shaken, the two men left the house and, shortly after, sent for a minister.

The minister entered the cellar, invoked the Holy Trinity and, with the words "Little red man, go to rest," exorcised Brother Andreas Kremser's spirit. He was never seen again; the Little Red Man, however, continues to haunt the imagination. For the people of Winston-Salem, he really has never left.

The Legend of Blackbeard

Ocracoke Inlet, on the eastern coast of North Carolina, is perhaps the longest-lived inlet on the Outer Banks and has the notorious distinction of being one of the favorite haunts of legendary pirate Edward Teach, affectionately and better known as Blackbeard.

Edward Teach was born in Bristol, England sometime in the late 17th century. He was a burly giant of a man: 6 feet 4 inches from head to toe, with a weight of 250 pounds. His hair was long and as black as pitch, its tresses braided into pleats and decorated with ribbons of varying colors. His black beard covered his entire face. Before battle, he would light slow-burning fuse cords dipped in saltpeter and lime-water and hang them from the brim of his hat. The wisps of smoke that circled his head only added to his already monstrous appearance. He truly was a hellish-looking creature, armed with a bandolier of six pistols across his chest and daggers and his cutlass hanging menacingly from his belt.

Blackbeard was the most notorious pirate to sail the Atlantic Coast of colonial America, attacking merchant ships up and down the coast from New England to the Virgin Islands without mercy. Anchored close to shore at Ocracoke aboard the *Queen Anne's Revenge*, Blackbeard could watch, unseen, as merchant ships passed by his vantage point. With a cry, he would rally his crew to bear down upon their unsuspecting prey. Many a merchant captain cowered in fear as Blackbeard's flag, a macabre image of a horned skeleton holding fish bones in one hand and a spear from which hung a bleeding red heart in the other, flew up its mast.

Blackbeard truly was a hellish-looking creature, armed with a bandolier of six pistols across his chest.

Blackbeard had gotten his start as a privateer in the early 18th century, during the War of the Spanish Succession. England, desperate to stop the flow of gold and silver that Spanish galleons bore from the Americas, gave sailors on certain private ships license to pillage. But when the war ended in 1713, these privateers, enamored with this lawless existence, continued their work and turned their cannon upon any ships carrying valuable goods.

Because he was close with Charles Eden, the royal governor of North Carolina who turned a blind eye to Blackbeard's activities in exchange for a share of his plunder, Blackbeard made his home in the Outer Banks. Its shallow waters and labyrinth-like network of inlets rendered it a virtual pirate's paradise, a hedonistic Eden from which pirates could refit and rest in peace.

Blackbeard grew wealthy from his plunders and for a while, in 1718, actually appeared to have retired to the quiet village of Bath, where he enjoyed a pampered and privileged lifestyle socializing with Governor Eden and the local elite. Blackbeard even acquired a level of celebrity, one no doubt enhanced by the fact that he often chose to sell his plunder to the public at reasonable prices. But within months, Blackbeard had nearly exhausted his funds and turned once more to the seas to support the lavish lifestyle to which he'd become accustomed. Eden continued to turn a blind eye.

There were those, however, who had grown weary of Blackbeard's piracy. Among them was the governor of Virginia, Alexander Spottswood. In November 1718, Spottswood dispatched a contingent of the British Royal Navy to North Carolina with orders to capture or to kill Blackbeard. *Jane* and *The Ranger* sailed out under the command of Lieutenant Robert Maynard for the southern tip of Ocracoke Island. Blackbeard, aboard *The Adventure,* watched the two ships approach and decided to lure them into a narrow channel, beneath which lurked a hidden sandbar.

Jane and *The Ranger* grounded themselves upon the bar and Blackbeard roared with delight. "Damn you villains, who are you?" he yelled. "Whence come you?"

Maynard, thoroughly piqued for having fallen so clumsily into the trap, held his ground. "You can see from our colors, we are no pirates," he retorted. Blackbeard demanded that Maynard sail out on his ship's yawl, but Maynard refused. "I cannot spare my boat, but I will come aboard you as soon as I can with my sloop," Maynard shouted. The threat, which seemed idle and utterly futile given Maynard's position, only enraged Blackbeard.

"Damnation seize my soul if I give you mercy or take any from you," the pirate cried out. With a nod, *The Adventure*'s crew mobilized itself, brandishing their pistols and cutlasses, eager to taste blood once more.

Maynard, undaunted, retorted, "I expect no mercy from you. Nor shall I give any!" He ordered his men to toss water barrels over the side and a stunned Blackbeard watched as the two sloops freed themselves from the sandbar. The ships exchanged gunfire as *The Adventure* maneuvered itself next to Maynard's ship. With a cry, the pirates leapt from their deck to Maynard's, cutlasses glinting in the sun.

As curly wisps of smoke enveloped Blackbeard's head, he cut his way to Maynard. Brandishing his pistol, he fired a shot that went astray. Maynard turned and fired; though his aim was true, Blackbeard didn't even stagger. He lurched forward, jabbing with his sword. Maynard, stunned, traded blows with the notorious pirate but found himself retreating from Blackbeard's hammering blows. With a dull clatter, Maynard's blade fell from its hilt. Blackbeard had shattered the weapon. With a wicked grin, Blackbeard raised his blade high above his head, ready to cleave Maynard's body in two.

To Maynard's rescue came his men, who rallied quickly around the fallen lieutenant. One man drew his sword across

Blackbeard's neck, and blood gushed from an open wound. While such a wound might have felled a lesser man, it only gave Blackbeard a moment to pause. Gamely, he rallied his men and continued to fight. Maynard's men fell upon the giant. In the melee, Blackbeard was shot five times and cut deeply at least another 20. Finally, to the eternal shock of his mates, Blackbeard staggered across the deck, life ebbing from him as surely as the blood that seeped from his many wounds. He collapsed to his knees and, falling forward, breathed his last breath. Blackbeard was dead.

Triumphant, Maynard lopped of Blackbeard's head and hung it from the bow of his ship. The body he ordered cast overboard. According to legend, when Blackbeard's body hit the water, it didn't sink immediately. Instead, the decapitated body circled the ship a full three times before finally sinking to its watery tomb. Maynard left the head suspended from his bowsprit for weeks, allowing it to rot in the damp heat as a warning to other pirates. Legend holds that his skull was made into a silver-plated cup.

Today, the villagers of Ocracoke Island, who have transformed the place into a virtual living monument to the once-feared pirate, boast that Blackbeard still roams the waters of the Outer Banks. Cock an ear toward Pamlico Sound and you might hear the sounds of gunfire cracking through the air. When the sun rises and the Atlantic turns pink and orange with the approach of dawn, a ship will pull out of the misty Ocracoke Inlet, silhouetted against the horizon. Flying high above the deck is Blackbeard's *Jolly Roger*, whipping and snapping in the breeze. The ghost ship of Blackbeard glides across the waters, silent as a cloud, and, for a moment, Blackbeard lives again.

Captain Harper's Ghostly Aide

The year was 1897. As the winds and rains of a great Atlantic winter storm lashed the deck of his steamer, Captain John C. Harper, his coat pulled tightly across his chest, stepped out from the pilot house. He peered up at the skies and saw nothing but a black and gray mass of dark clouds that promised more of the same to come. With a sigh, he wiped the rain from his face and headed back into the pilot house.

Wearily, he sat back down across from his ferry's sole passenger, a talkative Scot whose thick Gaelic burr was only matched by his loquaciousness. The man had been nattering in his ear since the steamer had pulled away from the port at Wilmington, bound for Smithville, and the minute Harper stepped back into the warmth of the room, the Scot had started up chatting again. Harper almost preferred the howling wind and pounding rain to this passenger, who seemed intent on regaling Harper with tales of one maritime disaster after another.

"So, as I was saying," the passenger continued, "my grandfather's father. He came to America before it was even America. Them limeys captured my ancestor with two other Highlanders. Clapped them in them chains, they did, and threw them in a cell in Brunswick Town."

Harper sighed and poured himself another stiff shot of rum, wishing he could be down below with his crew who were no doubt taking advantage of the light work to help themselves to more than their fair ration of the stuff.

"Well," the passenger continued, "things looked bad. The redcoats—they wanted to string up the three of them for conspiring with the colonials. So they loaded them up on a boat, but then a great storm rose up." The Scot peered out at the rain-spattered window and nodded his head. "Much like this one, I'd imagine," he said with a laugh. "The storm came and my great grandfather, well, he took off. Managed to put out to sea in a small lifeboat, promised to get help. He died that night, went straight down to Davy Jones' locker that night." The Scot paused dramatically, as if waiting for some sort of acknowledgement or encouragement. None was forthcoming. The Scot continued. "The damndest thing. Isn't it?"

Captain Harper rubbed his temples slowly. *First the storm and now this man*, he thought to himself darkly. The story was far from entertaining and certainly seemed wholly inappropriate considering the circumstances. Silence fell upon the room for a blissful moment, accompanied only by the staccato pitter-patter of rain falling upon the pilot house roof. But then, with a great shudder and jarring crash, the steamer ran hard aground upon a shoal, just opposite of old Brunswick Town.

The Scot peered again out the window. "Well, whaddya know?" he said to no one in particular. Captain Harper was already out of the room, darkly cursing his passenger. He leaned forward, looking down at the prow of his steamer and realized with a sinking dread that while the ship was fine, he'd have to wait until the tide came in to free the craft.

With great reluctance, Captain Harper returned to the pilot house. "We'd best get below decks, sir," he informed his passenger. "We'll catch our deaths from the cold up here waiting for the tide." The two clambered down below and set to waiting. Captain Harper noticed that the initial terror of the collision had silenced the Scot's tongue.

Harper nursed his patience with a small glass of rum and offered what remained in the bottle to his passenger, who looked as if he'd had a sudden attack of seasickness. The cabin door burst open with a great clatter. One of Harper's deckhands rushed into the room, his hair and clothes soaked through. Through chattering teeth, he frantically recounted what he'd just seen.

"Captain, Captain," he said breathlessly, "there's something up there. At least I think so."

Captain Harper stared at the man curiously. "I don't know if I get your meaning," Harper returned.

"I seen him. I seen a man up there." The deckhand pointed gingerly with one finger toward the deck. "He looked like he was in great pain and he was an absolute mess. He was holding to the railing, sir, and then, he raised one arm and with one bony finger, he pointed into the darkness. I went to see to him but…" The deckhand trailed off, almost as if afraid to even describe what happened next.

"But what?" Harper demanded. "You going to tell me what happened next or would you like me to hazard a guess?"

The deckhand took a deep breath. "I reached out to him, sir," he said quietly and haltingly. "But when I touched his arm, he just…vanished. Like he'd walked into a fogbank." The Scot listened intently, which Harper found extremely annoying. The captain stood up and put his mouth next to the crewman's ear.

"You go sober up now," he whispered. "Dry off, get some rest. And not a word of this to anyone, you understand?" The deckhand nodded and scurried away.

A short time later the tide finally began to shift and, slowly but surely, Harper's steamer managed to free itself from the shoal. Harper bounded back up to the deck, determined to reach Smithville as quickly as he could. He made his way to the pilot house but then, somewhere from the darkness, he heard what was unmistakably a human cry of distress. Harper and his crew rushed to the railing and saw below them what looked like two figures, more skeletons than men, manacled and chained to an old rowing barge.

"Ropes," Harper barked. "Quickly now." His crew threw ropes over the side but as they watched the cables twist and turn in the wind, the barge and its passengers vanished, as if swallowed up by the darkness itself. Harper reset his course, determined to follow the barge. Very soon, the steamer came across a capsized ship. Clinging to its remains were two men, struggling to fight back the dark, icy waters of the Atlantic. Harper's crew rescued the two men, the only survivors of a riverboat crew of seven. The spooked deckhand couldn't help but tell his captain that the direction in which they had sailed was exactly along the path his ghost had pointed out.

Harper wasn't so quick to dismiss his crewman this time. The events of the evening had struck him as oddly familiar— the grounding of their ship near old Brunswick Town, the ghost on the deck, the two emaciated men manacled to the barge and then the rescue of two others; it all reminded him of the story his Scottish passenger had told him. The captain brought the passenger and deckhand together and asked the latter to describe the apparition he had seen. He did so and when he was finished, the Scot was certain that the man the deckhand had just described could have been no one other than his long-dead great-grandfather.

Harper's ferry finally pulled into Smithville a short time later. Harper knew he would never forget the events of that stormy night. He repeated the story often, usually on a dark and stormy night, fully convinced that what he had witnessed was incontrovertible proof of the existence of ghosts. "It was the Scot's ancestor and his two friends come to life," he'd say. "I'm sure of it. He meant to help us help them." The three Highlanders may have not been able to save themselves, but they clearly mean to help others avoid their same tragic fates.

Reed Gold Mine

Mention "gold rush" anywhere in North America and you'll more than likely stir up associations with California, Colorado, the Black Hills and the Klondike, and tales of waters so rich with the metal that all a man needed to do to strike it rich was plunge his hands in a creek. But as legendary as the gold rushes of the West were, the mine that started it all was not at Cherry Creek, Colorado or at Sutter's Mill, California. America's first gold rush took place just outside of Charlotte, North Carolina, on a homestead known as the Reed Farm. The Reed Gold Mine today is a tourist site, its reserves of gold long ago exhausted. But lurking deep within its preserved shafts is the specter of a long-dead miner who was driven insane years ago by the untimely death of his wife, and who is still hard at work, hoping to find the nugget that will finally allow him to rest.

The Reed Gold Mine, America's first, might never have even existed. In 1799, farmer John Reed's son, Conrad, brought home a hunk of a heavy yellow metal that he claimed he found in Little Meadow Creek. Unaware of the stone's value, Reed used the 17-pound "rock" as a doorstop. For three years, it sat upon the Reed homestead floor until finally Reed took it to a Fayetteville jeweler. The jeweler was stunned. The doorstop was pure gold, and he offered to buy it from Reed for whatever price Reed named. The naïve Reed asked for three dollars and fifty cents. He later learned that its actual worth was closer to 1000 times what he'd been paid. The 17-pound doorstep was worth 3600 dollars.

The Linker Adit - entrance to the mine tunnels

Reed, thoroughly piqued, maintained an even disposition. He knew there were other yellow rocks out there in his Little Meadow Creek and, with three partners who supplied the capital and equipment, he began prospecting. They quickly became profitable and in 1803, a slave recovered a 28-pound nugget at Little Meadow Creek. Their success set off a gold rush, and people from all over poured into the state, eager to get their hands on the flakes and nuggets of gold. Charlotte, 20 miles away, saw its population rocket as a number of other mines, like Parker and Harris, opened. North Carolina became known as the "golden state." Before 1828, all gold minted by the government came from North Carolina and for 50 years, the state led the nation in gold production.

Reed Gold Mine continued to prosper, but after years of placer and creek mining, panning was no longer as lucrative as it once had been. In 1831, after an assayer confirmed that the land was indeed replete with white quartz rock and the gold that often appeared with it, Reed Gold Mine's first mine shaft was sunk.

Eleanor Mills, a neighbor of the Reeds, watched it all happen with a mixture of envy and disgust. She'd seen the Reeds' wealth grow by leaps and bounds, and bitterly felt that her husband, though decent and kind, was far too simple and listless. As Mrs. Reed paraded around Charlotte and Fayetteville in the latest fashions, in gowns of taffeta and silk, Eleanor Mills was still wearing the plain and tattered dresses she'd bought as a newlywed. At first, she'd gently prodded her husband, Eugene, subtly suggesting that he buy a pan and a screen and make his fortunes on a stake. Instead, he dismissed all her hints with a simple smile and nod, only to return to the boomtowns that had sprung up all around like noxious weeds, to while away his hours in the saloons and poker joints.

Eleanor's objections became more vocal and strident, and she resembled less a doting wife than a raging harpy. When Eugene could tolerate it no longer, he finally resolved to ask John Reed for a job working the mine shafts of the Upper and Lower Hills. Reed, always grateful for more help, agreed and Eugene was soon quarrying away in the mines, chiseling out milky white chucks of quartz and tossing them by the handful beneath the huge, grinding wheels that crushed the stones to liberate the gold within.

There it was—that screech of his wife, nagging him, demanding him to work hard.

The work was arduous, an ill fit for Eugene's easygoing and lazy temperament. But, despite all her complaints, he did love his wife and was determined to please her. If she wanted a fortune in gold, then she'd have it. Initially mollified, Eleanor quickly returned to her nagging ways, insisting that Eugene work harder. The two often argued well into the evening, their strident voices ringing through the night.

Eugene rarely smiled now, and he plodded through his days with a permanent frown etched upon his gaunt face. But as hard as he worked, it never seemed to be enough for Eleanor. One evening, the two were mired, yet again, in an argument. Eleanor was in a mood that night and let loose with a verbal barrage that called into question, among other things, Eugene's manhood. It was more than the man could take. The formerly passive Eugene, once so apathetic and dispassionate, was spurred to action. Blinded by his fury, he pushed his wife away from him, not realizing that she stood precariously near the edge of the staircase.

As she staggered back from his shove, her feet got tangled within the hem of her long dress and, with a shriek, she reeled down the staircase, dashed her head against a beam and collapsed upon the floor in a raggedy heap. Eugene, aghast, raced down the steps and cradled his wife in his arms. Her breathing was ragged, and blood was already beginning to pool beneath her cracked head. The shock was so great that Eugene fainted.

When he finally came to, Eugene was startled to hear a very familiar sound. Though his wife lay where she had fallen, and it was obvious that she was dead, her voice—that awful, shrill, strident tone that was about as gentle as fingers raked across a blackboard— was ringing in his ears. He sat up with a start and scurried across the landing as quickly as he could, staring at the body with eyes wide as saucers.

He closed his eyes and covered his ears, but still, there it was—that screech of his wife, nagging him, demanding him to work hard, to earn a great fortune and liberate her from this hardscrabble life. Though he had been stricken by a moment of grief, it quickly passed as Eugene paced around his house, yelling at the corpse on his floor to shut up. Finally, the voice having bored a hole in his sanity, Eugene trussed the body up, loaded it upon a sled and dragged Eleanor to the Reed Gold Mine shaft, her voice in his ears the entire way. With a grunt, he dragged the body to what he hoped was an abandoned shaft and tossed it down.

When he returned to his home, he swore that he could still hear her. As the days and nights passed, Eugene's sanity grew more tenuous. He'd invite complete strangers into his home, repeatedly asking them if they could hear his wife. None of them did. The only thing that seemed to ameliorate his condition was toiling in the mines and Eugene worked all his waking hours to escape his demons. He muttered to himself constantly and soon grew thin and haggard. Eugene died shortly after his wife; he'd worked himself to death.

Not long after, people began whispering that they could hear a terrifying shriek emanating from one of the mine shafts. Others claimed they could sense a heavy and oppressive presence in the tunnels working alongside them. When Eleanor's body was finally recovered, people realized what had happened to her. As for Eugene, miners were convinced that it was his spirit down in the shafts, determined still to exorcise his demons.

By the mid-19th century, the gold boom of North Carolina had come to an end. The gold strikes of Sutter's Mill in California led to a great westward migration, and many in the shafts of North Carolina went too. Though Reed Gold Mine continued to operate until 1912, its glory days were in the past. Though time and history may have passed the mine by, the spirits of Eugene and Eleanor Mills continue to linger beneath the earth, attractions of the site's annual ghost tours. Her shrieks still echo through the night as Eugene toils alongside her.

4
Public
Phantoms

The Pink Lady

On July 9, 1912, near the North Carolina city of Asheville and beneath the rugged panorama of the mist-shrouded Blue Ridge Mountains, Edwin W. Grove watched with satisfaction as the ground was finally broken on a plan he'd first envisioned in 1909. Grove had been the owner and founder of the highly profitable Grove's Pharmacy and Paris Medical Company in St. Louis, Missouri. On the advice of his doctor, Grove began spending his summers in Asheville in the late 19th century, in hopes that the pleasant climate might alleviate his bronchitis. Asheville proved restive not only to his body, but also to his soul. In 1909, standing on the sun-kissed grassy slopes of Sunset Mountain, Grove beheld an awesome sight: a stunning view of North Carolina's famed Blue Ridge Mountains. Inspired, Grove began formulating plans to build a resort hotel. In the words of his son-in-law, Fred Seely, he planned "to build a big home where every modern convenience could be found…with all the old-fashioned qualities of genuineness with no sham." Three years later, the empty hillside became host to a flurry of construction as engineers using mules, wagons, pulleys, and ropes hoisted hulking monoliths of Sunset Mountain granite, some weighing as much as 10,000 pounds, into place. Within a year, the Grove Park Inn Resort was open for business. It was an immediate success; guests were rendered speechless by the majestic views and impeccable service steeped in Old World charm.

Notable guests over the years have included F. Scott Fitzgerald, author of *The Great Gatsby,* who stayed in rooms 441 and 443 while his wife underwent treatment in nearby

Asheville's Highland Hospital. Other famous names include Will Rogers, Thomas Edison, Hungarian composer Béla Bartók, American composer George Gershwin, Franklin and Eleanor Roosevelt and seven other American presidents. But for all its star wattage, its amenities (including a 40,000 square-foot spa and a golf course designed by Donald Ross), its attentive staff and its rustic opulence, the Grove Park Inn Resort is perhaps best known for a lone ethereal guest. Her name was forgotten long ago, and today she is known simply as the Pink Lady of Grove Park. Many guests have wished to linger at the Grove Park Inn; only the Pink Lady does. She first checked into the hotel in 1920 and, if the accounts are to be believed, she has tarried there for over eight decades.

In 1920, a young, beautiful woman clad in a flowing pink gown that conjured rosy sunsets fell from the fifth floor to the Palm Court Atrium below. It was dismissed as a suicide, though no one knows for sure. What is more certain is that in death, this guest has attained an immortality and fame belying her humble origins.

Ever since her body was discovered crumpled on the atrium floor, the Pink Lady has appeared to guests and employees of the Grove Park Inn. Sometimes she is nothing more than a cloud of thick pink smoke (one guest described it as a "pinkish pastel that just flows"). Other times she is a fully realized (though transparent) figure in a diaphanous pink gown; most of her thick, lustrous blonde hair is swept up from her face, with a few stray tresses left dangling to frame her beauty. Even when not seen, the Pink Lady makes her presence felt, whether through tickling the feet of unsuspecting guests, giving a quick warm embrace, riding empty elevators or turning lights on and off. Hers is a benevolent, though often mischievous, spirit. Of course, not everyone is a fan. In the 1950s, a painter allegedly tried to enter room 545 and was subjected to such a severe blast of cold air that he never attempted it again. Even now, some employees refuse to enter the room.

For years, Grove Park Inn refused to acknowledge her existence, despite the hundreds of eyewitness accounts that spoke to the contrary. It wasn't until 1995 that the establishment, in the face of overwhelming evidence (albeit anecdotal and unsubstantiated), relented and sought out the assistance of researchers. They hired Joshua P. Warren, a noted local writer, filmmaker and paranormal enthusiast who founded the League of Energy Materialization and Unexplained phenomena Research (L.E.M.U.R.). Warren's investigation took months. Working with a team that included Mark-Ellis Bennett, Tim VanDenBerghe and Tim Pedersen, he pored over the hotel's history, interviewed countless eyewitnesses, probed every nook and cranny of the place and stayed in a number of rooms—though none matched the energy and power of room 545. His meticulous research pointed toward a conclusion many had already suspected. The Grove Park Inn was indeed haunted by a Pink Lady. As a guest, she must have stayed in room 545 on the night of her death.

Since Warren's investigation, the Grove Park Inn has embraced the Pink Lady; its staff members share their personal experiences and have even cobbled together a guide on her history. Curious guests often request to stay in 545, specifically with the intention of catching a glimpse of her. One couple brought a video camera for their stay, hopeful that they might be able to catch the Pink Lady on tape. They began taping as soon as they stepped onto the fifth floor, narrating their progress to the room. When they watched the tape later, they were puzzled to find that while their walk to 545 had been captured as expected, all footage inside the room had been replaced with nothing but static. The stories rise up thick and fast, all but guaranteeing that a stay at the Grove Park Inn will be quite unlike any other.

Take, for example, Patty Glatz (not her real name) and her experience with the Pink Lady. Patty, 15 years old, recently stayed at the inn and, given her young age, it's not surprising that she found her encounter with the Pink Lady absolutely terrifying. While staying in Asheville with her basketball team, Patty, tired from the uncomfortable bus ride, decided to go to sleep instead of going out with her teammates. At about nine o'clock in the evening, she rode the elevator up to the fourth floor. She walked to her room, took out her key card and then felt compelled to turn around.

"I felt as if someone was watching me," she says. "It was really eerie and strange." Standing behind her was a very tall, very attractive woman with blonde hair and dressed in a "really really old, long and pink dress." There was something pitiful about the woman who just stood by the railing, looking out over the atrium. "I asked her if she was okay," Patty recalls, "but she just stood there, looking down." It was then that Patty noticed something she hadn't before: the woman was transparent. "I could see right through her to the other side," Patty says. With a gasp, Patty dropped her key card and watched as the woman leaned over the edge, perching precariously on the tips of her toes. "Then," Patty continues, "she just vanished into the air." Patty thought the woman had fallen and ran over to the edge. She looked down but saw no one. A chill ran down her back.

Terrified, Patty picked up her key card, hurried into the room and made sure to lock the door behind her. Thinking some music might soothe her jangled nerves, Patty turned on the radio, turned the volume low and got into bed, pulling the covers tightly around her. She hadn't been sleeping long when she was roused from sleep by an explosion of noise—a big band playing swing music. "Something changed the station and turned up the volume," she says firmly. "No one else was in the room but me. My roommate hadn't come back yet and I was definitely alone." She screamed, to no one in particular, "Stop. Please stop!" The radio, thoroughly chastised, complied. The volume dropped and the pop music she'd been listening to mysteriously returned. Patty spent the rest of the night sleepless, tossing and turning in her bed.

Unlike Patty, most people with Pink Lady stories to tell come away intrigued and, to some extent, delighted. In an interview with Pete Zampras of Asheville's *Mountain Xpress*, (an online newspaper) Bob Farrar, a 51-year-old attorney from Georgia, recalls the time he got a hug from the Pink Lady. Bob had long been a firm skeptic when it came to the paranormal. He had been married for 22 years to a woman who claimed to have been raised in a haunted house. "I'd come up with logical explanations," he says. "I said [to her], 'You're absolutely crazy.'" He doesn't think she's so crazy anymore.

Farrar's conversion took place on November 27, 2001, when he stayed at the Grove Park Inn for the first time. The resort's spa had just opened and Farrar decided to treat himself to a session of polarity-massage therapy. As he was enjoying the service, he felt something peculiar. "I felt a very strong sense that someone gave me a gentle hug on my right shoulder," he says. "I felt them put their arms around my neck and squeeze. It was so real that it startled me...I opened my eyes to discover that [the therapist] was still working on my feet. I didn't see the Pink Lady, but I felt her presence. I'd swear [to it] under oath." Though he had been in trance-like state, the hug snapped him into full consciousness and he spent the next five minutes in the physical embrace of someone he knew had to be feminine; the touch was tender and warm.

Farrar reasons that the Pink Lady must have taken pity on him. Single and unattached, he was in a couple-massage room. The Pink Lady, Zampras writes, might have "felt bad about his lack of a lady friend." When asked whether he might have been under the influence of something chemical, Farrar responds, "I haven't had a drink in 17 years. I never took an illegal drug...I'm straight as they come."

Farrar states, "I tell you, I'm a believer now." The man who once questioned his ex-wife's sanity has now returned to the Grove Park Inn on numerous occasions, determined to seek the Pink Lady out. Lamentably, he's been unsuccessful thus far, but he would be well advised to practice patience. The Pink Lady keeps a busy schedule. He isn't the only guest to have caught the eye of the Pink Lady.

Katherine Sales remembers well her stay at the resort. She and her husband had come for a weekend to celebrate their 10th wedding anniversary, in July 2000. In the middle of the night, Katherine was roused from sleep by what she calls "strange sounds...as if somebody [was] walking across the floor." Peering into the darkness, she couldn't see anything and grabbed her husband's hand for comfort. Only it wasn't her husband's hand. The hand she was holding lay to her right; her husband was sleeping comfortably to her left. Katherine, eyes wide with shock, slowly turned to the right. "There was no one there," she recalls. "But I distinctly felt the physical sensation of someone holding my hand. It lingered for a moment and then it was gone." The next morning, the incident still very much on her mind, Katherine related her account to a front desk clerk. He laughed sympathetically and told her that she had nothing to worry about. "He said, 'It's only the Pink Lady. She likes to look in on our guests from time to time.'" Katherine, too, has returned to the Grove Park Inn in hopes of having another encounter. The Pink Lady certainly has a way about her.

Thalian Hall

The waterfront town of Wilmington, North Carolina is a peaceful, postcard-ready place, blessed with the natural beauty for which the state is famous. It was once the largest city in North Carolina, and many of its historic buildings hearken back to the time when politics, culture and society converged in this oceanside city. Among them is the beloved architectural relic known as Thalian Hall, which still serves as the centerpiece of the region's arts community. Should you be fortunate enough to catch a show at Thalian Hall, cast your gaze to the front row of the front balcony; you might just see a trio of dedicated actors who haven't let a little thing like their own mortality keep them away from the stage. Though the actors' appearances are sporadic, more than one stage manager or theater employee has reported walking through the empty auditorium to turn up the seats only to return later to find the three seats in the front row of the front balcony, stage center, down again. These are the reserved seats of the theater-loving dead.

Thalian Hall is a magnificent and stunning place. Words can barely do it justice. It's the sort of bedazzling place that induces awe—a stirring spectacle for both the eye and the soul. Plush seats draped in red and purple fabric sit silently in the shadow of an arched grand stage. The stage boasts friezes of red and gold and Corinthian columns reminiscent of ancient Greece. The long, sweeping balcony's soft and graceful curves flow across the auditorium as supple as a wave from the Atlantic. It is supported by alabaster columns along which creep intricately detailed vines, and it proved so inspirational and moving that a version of it was copied for use in Washington's Ford Theatre. It is little wonder that the place provokes such a hushed response; it was designed by John Montague Trimble, one of America's foremost 19th-century theater architects. Thalian Hall is his only surviving theater, and what a precious thing it is.

Constructed between 1855 and 1858 by an army of highly skilled African Americans (it's made clear that some were slaves, while others were not) Thalian Hall originally had room for 1000 patrons. It was named for the Thalian Association, a community theater group that has been operating since 1788 and remains the country's oldest. Thalian Hall quickly became a regular and mandatory stop for national touring artists during the Civil War. Throughout its history, it played host to luminaries such as Lillian Russell, Buffalo Bill Cody, John Philip Sousa, Joseph Jefferson, Maurice Barrymore (scion of the great Barrymore acting clan and grandfather of actress Drew Barrymore) and Sir Henry Lauder. It also served as the host for local concerts, recitals, graduations and exhibitions.

During the early 20th century, with the end of the great days of touring road shows, Thalian Hall suffered. Attendance dropped precipitously and the hall flirted with demolition as so-called progressives cried out for something more modern. But Wilmington, which, as a community, has always demonstrated an instinct toward preservation, repeatedly rallied around the institution and saved it time and time again from the wrecking ball. A small fire in 1973 paved the way for the theater's restoration, and it reopened in 1975 to packed halls. In 1988, a $5 million renovation and expansion project began. The building reopened anew on March 2,

Thalian Hall is a magnificent and stunning place.

1990, to great acclaim and with its future secured. Through it all, the theater always had the support of the arts community, even those members who had long since passed away.

Thalian Hall is reportedly home to three spirits—actors who once graced Thalian Hall's stage in the early 20th century. They've been seen quite often; one of the liveliest and detailed accounts comes from a Mrs. William G. Robertson of Wilmington, whose story can be found at AmericanTerror.com. Robertson worked closely with the theater during the 1960s and often experienced what she called "strange sensations" and a "certainty that others were there [in addition] to ourselves" in the theater. As stage manager, Robertson spent many evenings at the hall watching over rehearsals and she became quite accustomed to the sensation that they were playing to an unseen audience. But then, during rehearsals for *Dial 'M' for Murder,* "things began to happen."

During one rehearsal, Robertson felt compelled, without knowing exactly why, to look up toward the first balcony. Initially, she saw nothing amidst the dark shadows but as her eyes adjusted, she gradually became aware that there were "three figures sitting in the first row of seats, stage center. There were two men and a lady." It was a startling sight to be sure, and wordlessly she motioned with a pointed finger for one of the cast members to look. He followed her gaze up toward the balcony and then walked over to her. "Do you see two men and a woman up there?" he asked.

Without turning away, Robertson nodded slowly, fearful that if she were to avert her gaze, they might vanish. The cast member, similarly transfixed, exclaimed, "Look at their clothes! They're dressed in Edwardian costumes! Let's go have a look." Robertson, with the entire cast in tow, hurried up to the balcony, excitement surging through her veins.

When they reached the balcony, it was empty. Many stood looking around, muttering in awe. They had all definitely seen three figures, so where could they have gone? The cast might have doubted what they'd seen if not for what they found in the front row. Every seat was turned up, except for three, stage center—the exact same seats where the two men and one woman had been sitting. Rehearsals, needless to say, broke early that night. The ghostly trio gave an encore performance several nights later when they appeared, in the same Edwardian dress, sitting in the same seats they'd occupied earlier.

To Robertson's eyes, they bore striking resemblances to three actors she was familiar with. Fanny Davenport was an acclaimed stage actress who had great successes with touring productions of Augustin Daly's *Pique* in 1877, Anna E. Dickinson's *An American Girl* in 1880 and Victorien Sardou's *Fédora* from 1883 to 1887. Richard Mansfield was arguably one of the greatest actors of the late 19th century (Yale professor and critic William Lyon Phelps called him "one of the greatest of modern actors and certainly the most intellectual"). He was responsible for introducing American audiences to George Bernard Shaw's *Arms and the Man* and *The Devil's Disciple* and Henrik Ibsen's epic *Peer Gynt*. Edwin Booth was one of the first great American actors, whose *Hamlet* ran for a legendary 100 nights at New York's Winter Garden Theater in 1864. His promising career came to a premature and scandal-ridden end when his younger brother, the notorious John Wilkes Booth, assassinated President Abraham Lincoln at Ford Theater in 1865. Whether or not

Cast your gaze to the front row of the first balcony; you might see a ghostly trio of dedicated actors.

these spirits are indeed those of these late actors isn't certain, since no one has ever gotten close enough to offer a definitive identification. What a trio they would make.

Robertson's closest encounter with the spirits occurred backstage during a performance. As stage manager, she was in charge of wardrobe, making sure that all costumes were ready for actors and actresses to change into between scenes and acts. During one play's run, Robertson recalls the torture of having to undress an actress and redress her in a Victorian-era dress "with dozens of tiny buttons down the front" in just three minutes. To hasten the process, Robertson usually made sure the dress was laid out on a chair with a precise set of buttons left undone. But one evening, she completely forgot.

With her stomach twisted into knots and panic urging her steps, she hurried to the actress' dressing room where quite the surprise awaited her. "I just couldn't believe my eyes. There it was," she said. "[The dress was] hanging over the back of a chair. Just the right number of buttons had been unbuttoned and the dress was all ready for [the actress] to jump into." Only Robertson herself ever touched the costumes, and no one would admit to preparing the dress. Robertson was left to conclude that one of the sympathetic spirits-in-residence, well aware of the intricacies and inner workings of the stage, had decided to lend not just an ear, but also a hand.

By all accounts, Thalian Hall is still the temporary home to a trio of ghostly actors who may have quit this earthly stage long ago, but who still, like the modern-day theater lover, find something valuable and precious in the craft. Thalian Hall is a temple to the arts; its ghosts, the embodiment of its legacy, are its patron saints.

The Haunted North Carolina State Capitol

In the 19th century, a flurry of government buildings went up across the United States. Most planners followed the lead of Washington, D.C., employing the Greek Revival architectural style that was in vogue at the time. Among the finest examples of these glorious buildings is the North Carolina State Capitol, one of the nation's best-preserved and finest representations of the Greek Revival style. The North Carolina State Capitol is far from being the largest or even the grandest building of its kind, but few buildings can match its preservation. The building largely appears as it did when it first opened its doors for public service in 1840. The stonework, the ornamental plaster and ironwork, the mahogany desks and chairs that grace the various offices and all but one marble mantel are original. The capitol is essentially a living, breathing museum. It's almost as if it had been plucked from the late 19th century and dropped into the 21st. Not surprisingly, it is also home to a complement of spirits and ghosts.

With the signing of the Treaty of Paris in 1783, the American Revolution was brought to an end. At the time, Raleigh consisted of little more than an idea and a plan. The city was just a few small streets that worked their way around five public squares. A building to house the fledgling legislature was erected in 1796, but it was small and terribly plain. It was upgraded in 1822 but in 1831, a clumsy construction worker burned the entire thing down to the ground.

In December 1832, a sum of $50,000 was appropriated for the construction of a new capitol on the site. This time, no expense would be spared in its construction. Legislators were going to give their Tar Heels a "noble monument" that would be an object of "just and becoming pride." They envisioned a cross-shaped building atop which would sit a central, domed rotunda. To execute the design, state legislators turned to the New York architectural firm of Ithiel Town and Alexander Jackson, who had just completed work on the Connecticut State Capitol in New Haven and were in the process of planning the state capitol in Indianapolis.

Appropriately enough, construction on the new state capitol commenced on the Fourth of July, 1833. It took seven years to complete. Work was slow as funds were repeatedly exhausted in order to import artisans from as far away as Scotland, and ironwork, chandeliers and other hardware from Philadelphia. In the end, when the dust had settled and the North Carolina State Capitol was finally completed, the seven years and $533,000 (a sum three-and-a-half times more than the state's total revenue for the year) that had been spent on its construction became only an afterthought.

As the home of the state Supreme Court, the governor and the General Assembly, it's not surprising that the capitol has become a reservoir of lingering spirits. In time, the state departments grew to a size that could no longer be accommodated by the capitol. It became necessary for the Supreme Court and State Library to vacate the premises in 1888, and in 1963, the General Assembly began meeting in the State Legislative Building. Only the governor and the lieutenant governor remained in the North Carolina State Capitol. Or so they believed.

The building still experiences its share of political squabbles. Long-dead politicians who once served in the capitol are still hard at work.

Mr. Jackson is a night watchman who worked in the capitol building for 12 years until his retirement in 1990. For the most part, his nights were rather uneventful, and the building rested as still and silent as a morgue. It's an apt description, as the capitol is haunted by the spirits of individuals who spent most of their living lives devoting their time and energies toward the betterment of the state. Their dedication has proven to be unflagging.

On occasion, Jackson's nightly rounds took unexpected turns into the paranormal. As he walked the wide halls, nightstick at his side and flashlight in hand, he'd stop and turn to look behind him, wondering how he could hear a door slam behind him moments after he'd closed and locked it. Could there be someone in the building with him? He would then turn, walk back to the door and, with a puzzled frown, note that the door was still locked. Perhaps someone was hiding behind it? After unlocking the door and fanning his flashlight across the darkened room, he'd shake his head and wonder if he'd been at the job for too long.

One night, Jackson was walking by the library when he heard what sounded like books falling from their shelves. Three times he heard the distinctive sound, but when searching the room he found nothing amiss. No books lay on the ground. What had he heard? He had no ready answer. Jackson quickly became accustomed to the unusual things that happened on his nightly rounds, but he still marveled at how the manually operated elevator traveled from floor to floor with no passengers. He no longer gaped in surprise at unbroken panes of glass that he swore he'd heard shattering. When he felt the sensation of a cold hand brushing the nape of his neck, he no longer jumped in fear. He began to find something soothing in the faint strains of gospel hymns that he heard echoing through the building. He would simply nod, smile and then turn back to his work. Whenever something bizarre happened, Jackson would just attribute it to "the saint." "You get used to something like that," he said in an interview with the Associated Press. "I think there's a couple of million dollars buried somewhere there and they're just trying to tell us where it was."

Sam Townsend, an administrator at the capitol who worked late into the evening as often as three times a week, became fast friends with night watchman Mr. Jackson. Jackson often regaled him with accounts of the saint and his activities. Townsend initially scoffed at the stories, dismissing them as nothing more than a pleasant diversion from his work. It wasn't long before Townsend truly understood that Jackson's tales weren't born of fiction.

One evening, Townsend was working in his office when he heard what sounded like someone walking down the hall from the committee room toward his little office. The loud footsteps stopped just outside his door. Townsend opened the door but saw nothing except an empty hallway stretching out before him. When work took him into the committee room, Townsend again heard the mysterious footsteps, only this time it sounded as if someone was right there in the room with him. Every time it occurred, Townsend could see quite clearly that he was alone. The footsteps relented when a copier was temporarily stored in the committee room, but they started up again as soon as the copier was moved into another office.

Townsend began to wonder if he would ever catch an actual glimpse of the meek apparition. He did. One evening when Townsend arrived at the capitol to work, he opened the door to the Senate chamber. His ears were alert for the footsteps that had become as routine as his two cups of black coffee with a bit of sugar. Standing in the doorway of the Senate chamber was a figure. Townsend gasped and stepped back in fright. His fear turned to amazement as he watched the figure dissolve. Within moments, Townsend was left standing in the Senate chamber alone, with nothing but his shadow for company.

Raymond Beck worked as a curator for the building in 1981 and one evening while working late, he too had an encounter with the capitol's unearthly host in the third-floor library. Having finished with some books that he'd taken down from the shelves, Beck collected them in his hands and walked over to the bookcase to put them back. They fell to the ground with a dull thud. Beck had dropped them, convinced that he had felt someone's icy, vise-like grip upon his shoulder. He could feel someone staring at him so intently it felt as if the unseen eyes were boring holes into his back. With great urgency, Beck bent down to the floor, casting quick glances right and then left, but he saw nothing except rows and rows of books bathed in inky shadows. He walked up and down the room, looking down aisle after aisle. He called out for the person who'd touched him to reveal him or herself, but only the echo of his voice reverberated through the room. Then, there was only silence. Beck realized with a dreadful certainty that he was the only person in the room.

The curator quickly packed up his papers, stuffed them in his briefcase and left the room. He had done enough work for the evening. Now, Beck avoids working late. In an interview with the Associated Press, he said, "To be honest, I've always made it a rule to be out of the building at quitting time. I've had enough of those strange vibes here that I don't like sticking around after it gets dark."

No one really knows who these spirits might be, but judging from the late hours they keep and their affection for the building, it's not unreasonable to theorize that they were individuals connected intimately with the North Carolina State Capitol. Perhaps the spirits, like Raymond Beck and Sam Townsend, preferred the quiet of the night and the emptiness of the building when doing the bulk of their work. But they are not the only ghosts haunting the capitol.

Stands of oak trees that were planted near the capitol many years ago harbor their own secrets. Visitors walking beneath the trees' canopy have been startled by what they claim could only be the sounds of pistol shots and screams. There was a time when the only honorable and legitimate means of settling a dispute between gentlemen was the duel. A favored locale for the practice was in the oak tree stands of the state capitol. Centuries later, some of these true Southern gentlemen are apparently still at it.

The Lodge on Lake Lure

Situated on the banks of majestic Lake Lure in Hickory Nut Gorge, about 30 miles southeast of Asheville, Lodge on Lake Lure is a sun-kissed slice of Eden, a near utopian blend of a rustic country inn and a cozy bed and breakfast. Guests seek out its comforts, whiling away their precious and fleeting liberation golfing, fishing, swimming and boating. Given its setting, its chestnut walls, vaulted ceiling and hand-hewn beams, the sweet perfume of the lakeshore breeze and its attentive staff, it's no surprise that the Lodge on Lake Lure boasts the presence of one guest who has simply chosen never to check out.

In August 1937, George Penn, a highway patrolman, was hot in the pursuit of two criminals. In the gloaming, he cornered them and drew his gun. With a steady hand, he aimed his gun at the criminals' backs and called to them to raise their hands above their heads. One did so slowly, but the other reached quickly into his jacket, pulled out a pistol and fired a fatal shot into Penn's chest. Penn winced; the searing kiss of the bullet dropped him to the ground. The two criminals fled, leaving Penn to die in a pool of his own blood.

The news devastated Penn's colleagues, family and friends. Determined not to forget the memory of his sacrifice, friends erected a lodge at Lake Lure in his honor. It would serve as a private retreat for state troopers and their families. It served that purpose for years until it was converted into a bed and breakfast. Though the inn has changed hands and undergone a few renovations, the one constant throughout the years has been George Penn. Not only is the

Lodge at Lake Lure a monument to the patrolman, it's also been his home for decades.

There are numerous accounts from amazed eyewitnesses who claim to have seen Penn's ghostly spirit roaming the halls of the lodge. His favorite room, according to those who know him best, is Room 4. Guests checking into the room have often found a surprise awaiting them. They open the door, drop their luggage and see Penn standing before them. "I think you're in the wrong room," stunned guests will say, at which point Penn nods, smiles and then proceeds to calmly and quietly walk through the wall. But just because he appears to have vacated the room doesn't mean he has. Camera-happy guests have reported leaving their cameras on the nightstand only to discover later, when their rolls of film have been developed, that someone or something spent the evening taking pictures of the slumbering guests.

In 1990, a couple named Sanier bought the Lodge on Lake Lure, unaware of its ghostly resident. According to writer Robin Warshaw, they operated the inn for the first few months without incident. But then one morning, a guest sauntered into the regal Great Room and approached Robin Sanier with whispers of a ghost in her room. During the evening, she had awoken to see a man pacing around her room. She assumed that he had entered the wrong room and told him so. The man left and the shocked guest watched as he paced up and down the hallway. Her husband, roused by the commotion, looked from his wife's wide-eyed stare to the closed and locked door. "What're you looking at?" he said.

"Don't you see him?" she asked. "He's right there." The husband looked again, but saw only a door. He laughed off her claims, but she continued to insist that she had seen the figure through the door.

When Robin Sanier related the story later to other guests, one of them took a keen interest in the account. Robin had omitted the room number but the guest looked at her knowingly and said, "It was Room 4, wasn't it?" Robin was stunned. It had been Room 4. "How did you know?" she inquired. The guest smiled and then said, "It happened to me too." Certain now that the incidents had to be related, Robin called the lodge's previous owner, Doris Nunn, who confirmed that the place was indeed haunted. In an interview with Warshaw, Nunn recalled her frustration with the ghost's pranks. He had been fond of hiding objects and slamming doors around her as she cleaned, and Nunn grew so irritated that she often took to scolding the ghost.

The Saniers themselves didn't experience Penn's presence firsthand until their first Christmas. Gathered with kith and kin in the dining room and its wondrous views of both the Blue Ridge Mountains and the shimmering waters of Lake Lure, they were regaling each other with stories of the bizarre incidents that they had heard so much about but had never experienced. Robin's daughter, Betsy, opined, "If there is a ghost, I wish he'd do something." Penn, spurred by this open invitation, promptly grabbed a glass from the buffet table and tossed it against a counter on the other side of the room. Betsy had gotten her wish. She would later see a potted plant fly across the room, seemingly of its own volition. For research, Warshaw spent a night in the famous Room 4 but laments that she saw and felt nothing unusual. Penn must have been otherwise occupied that evening.

The Brown Lady

In 1848, North Carolina's second Baptist school opened as the Chowan Baptist Female Institute, a four-year college for women. In 1910 the school was renamed Chowan College and in 1931 it began accepting male students. Originally, young women studied and took classes in the McDowell Columns building, constructed in 1851. It is now a registered national historical landmark and the home of the college's administrative offices.

Simply put, "The Columns" is a gorgeous building constructed with locally made bricks. Enormous white columns line the front of the three-story building, and a veranda and second-story balcony sprawl behind them. The building conjures up images of ancient Rome crossbred with the grandeur of the Southern plantation home. It's plain to see why it's a registered historical landmark and why, for over a century, the enigma known simply as the Brown Lady has called it home. Many students of note have passed through the halls of Chowan College, but the Brown Lady remains its most famous and beloved.

Her name, as is so often the case with such stories, has been lost, but her life is no less compelling. In the 1860s, the Brown Lady was just another face in the crowd, a student with simple hopes and dreams, and, like all Americans, psychically scarred by the great convulsive conflict known as the Civil War. When North Carolina seceded from the Union in 1861, young able-bodied men from all over the state cheered and then promptly departed for the front, determined to fight for and defend the Confederacy. Among them was the Brown Lady's true love.

Before he departed, the two pledged their undying love for each other and though she begged him to stay, he refused. As a patriot, he was bound by honor and duty to fight. As she watched him and a host of others march away from Murfreesboro, she found herself unable to join in the great merriment that accompanied their departure. Her love turned and offered her one last dazzling smile. With that, he was gone and she was left with a hopeful heart and a dreadful certainty that he would not return alive.

He had promised to write as often as he could, but weeks passed without any word from him. The Brown Lady's anxiety only grew, her dread nibbling away at her constitution like a parasite. One sunny afternoon, she finally received a letter. With trembling hands, she opened it and began to read. A terrible, wrenching howl went through the halls of the McDowell Columns building. The Brown Lady's one true love was dead.

The Brown Lady never recovered from the news. She grew ill, her skin drawing tight and gaunt around her bones. With each passing day, she plunged ever deeper into the abyss of her torment, and it wasn't long before she, too, was dead. How she shuffled off this mortal coil isn't known. Some say she killed herself—flung herself off the second-floor balcony or hanged herself. Others say she died of her broken heart.

Not long after her death, students and staff began reporting mysterious encounters with a misty figure clad in a brown dress. She brushed past people in the halls and walked across freshly fallen snow without leaving a single track. They saw her in the halls and around the building and heard her

"The Columns" conjures images of ancient Rome and Southern plantation homes.

banging on the water pipes. Her friends knew that the Brown Lady had returned to Chowan College. When the McDowell Columns building was converted for use as the college's administrative offices, janitorial staff found that despite their best efforts, they could never keep the place clean. They would leave the building at night, its halls freshly swept and mopped, only to return in the morning to find leaves and twigs scattered everywhere.

In time, the Brown Lady became a beloved and durable part of campus lore. Indeed, in the 1940s and 1950s, Chowan College hosted Brown Lady Festivals for which a female student was chosen to dress up as the Brown Lady. She would lead a procession from the campus across the ravine to the Wise Family Cemetery. It was hoped that the Brown Lady's spirit, now inextricably linked with that of Chowan College, would imbue incoming students with pride and high idealism.

Tara Spears, who attended Chowan College in the 1990s, can't say that her encounter with the Brown Lady imbued her with much of anything except a minor case of the jitters. Tara was on her own one Saturday night in her dormitory. "I felt a little like a nerd," she says. "Pretty much everyone had either gone back home or were out boozing it up." But with her grades slipping, Tara was determined to bring her recent skid to a stop. "I had some exams coming up," she remembers, "and I had to study." So Tara sat beneath the sickly glow of her solitary desk lamp, poring over her notebooks. Studying is hard work and feeling a little peckish and thirsty, Tara decided to get a drink and a snack from the vending machines down the hall.

She got up, counted out her change and walked toward her door. As she put her hand on the knob, she heard a knock on the door. With a frown, Tara opened the door and peered out into the hallway. No one was there. She looked down the hall to the right, then the left, just in time to see a figure, shrouded in mist and draped in a brown dress, motioning for her to follow. "I thought I'd been studying too much," Tara laughs. She rubbed her eyes a few times and still the Brown Lady stood there beckoning. The Brown Lady then faded from view, like a Polaroid in reverse. Tara made a quick decision. She grabbed her books, stuffed them into her backpack and headed across campus to study at a friend's dorm. "Hell yes, it freaked me out," she says. "I'd never seen anything like that before. It was surreal and bizarre and creepy all at the same time."

Tara's roommate returned the following Sunday evening and Tara cautiously asked her whether or not she had ever seen anything strange in the dorm. "Like what?" her roommate answered slowly.

"Oh, I don't know," Tara answered. "Like a ghost?" Her roommate fairly exploded. She too had seen the apparition. Tara was relieved and soon discovered that many of her floor-mates had seen the Brown Lady too. Tara saw the Brown Lady many more times after that night and quickly became accustomed to her presence. "I may have overreacted a bit that first time," she admits with a laugh, "By the end of the year, we'd adopted her as a floor-mate."

Kara Cornell, who also attended Chowan College in the late 1990s, encountered the Brown Lady as well; her first experience was decidedly less shocking. Kara, a visual arts student, spent much of her time working on the theater productions that were performed in the McDowell Columns building. "I would work late," she says, "and one of my first nights, I heard something really odd. It sounded like someone was banging on the water pipes that run through the building." Kara remembers being startled by it and when she asked about the sound, her question was met with knowing glances and some gentle laughter. Indignant, Kara asked what was so funny. "Oh nothing," people answered, "it's just the Brown Lady, that's all." Throughout her four years at the college, Kara often heard the strange banging sound and remembers one time when, as a senior, she was working with a freshman who was startled by the sound. With wide eyes, he asked Kara what had happened. Kara laughed gently and said, "That's just the Brown Lady."

One of the more apocryphal accounts of the Brown Lady paints her as a defender of the college's female students. It seems that one night a student was walking across campus back to her dormitory. A man jumped out of the shadows, pushed her to the ground and began to attack her. But then, inexplicably, he fled. The student, grateful and relatively unharmed, fled to the safety of her dorm wondering what exactly had happened. She had been at his mercy and instead, he ran. With her description of the attacker, authorities were able to track down the assailant quickly.

When he was brought in for questioning, they found that his body bore all manner of bruises and welts. Authorities assumed that the young victim had inflicted the marks, but the man offered a different version of what had happened. "It was a lady in a brown dress," he said. "She did this to me." He claimed that someone had choked him and had also punched him in the chest, knocking the wind out of him. The girl didn't recall either choking or punching the man and he continued to insist that a lady in a brown dress had been his attacker. The students of Chowan College are certain that the Brown Lady had come to the girl's rescue.

Chowan College students speak often and fondly of their Brown Lady. There's a distinct sense of pride that creeps into their voices when they describe their experiences. The Brown Lady, whose academic career at Chowan College now spans three centuries, must surely feel more welcome than ever.

Tijuana Fats

Popular with both tourists and Blowing Rock locals, Tijuana Fats, a Mexican eatery, sits along a stretch of downtown's Main Street once home to a host of Mexican restaurants that sprawled from the mountains to the beach. At first glance, its tiled roof and stuccoed walls that peeked from behind a veil of ivy appear oddly incongruous with the trappings of this Appalachian resort town. But step inside, and Tijuana Fats' brightly colored walls of coral and aqua—decorated with multi-hued serapes and renderings of Pancho Villa and Zapata—and its lovingly crafted chestnut flooring cradle diners in an atmosphere both cozy and casual. Mosaics of tile adorn the tabletops; tin lamps hang from the ceiling. Animated conversations, lubricated by the ubiquitous margaritas, thrum and throb. It matters little whether you're a friend or a stranger; Tijuana Fats is a communal and friendly sort of place. Visit once and you may, like a certain spirited little girl, never want to leave.

Aside from offering the usual Mexican fare of chimichangas, tostadas, enchiladas and fajitas, Tijuana Fats also boasts the presence of the impish and mischievous spirit staff have baptized Mary. Look to the restaurant's fireplace, then cast your gaze down to its slate hearth and you'll see a most curious thing: a tiny, plain footprint pressed into the solid stone. Locals claim that it must be Mary's. Nothing less than the supernatural could leave such an impression on solid slate. It's truly an amazing oddity but such is the awe and wonder that Mary inspires. For 20 years, locals and tourists have marveled at the tiny footprint. For the same

20 years, Mary has been Tijuana Fats' constant resident. Long before Tijuana Fats even opened, the building it occupies served, alternatively, as a residence, a boutique and a restaurant. According to local lore, when it was a home, it nearly went up in flames. The building was saved, but not before the conflagration claimed the life of the family's young daughter, Mary.

Mitzi Darden, owner and operator of Tijuana Fats, speaks fondly of her resident spirit. In an interview with Leigh Ann Henion of nearby Boone's *Mountain Times*, Darden spoke of how she sees Mary as "just another member of her restaurant family." In fact, when the Yuletide rolls around, Darden, despite other staffers' reluctance, insists on hanging a stocking for Mary from the fireplace. Darden understands her staff's hesitation; they haven't spent as much time with Mary as she has and therefore are "fascinated and afraid at the same time... it's the unknown." Tijuana Fats' staff could be forgiven for their reluctance to embrace Mary as firmly and fully as Darden. She does have a way of spooking people.

Not long ago, the general manager briefly left the dining room. When he returned, he stared in amazement at the ceiling where every single lamp was swaying in unison, like a grand metronome. With only one other person in the restaurant, the general manager knew that what he was seeing was not some prank, but Mary at work. She's quite fond of the lamps; if they're not swinging back and forth in concert, they're spinning. Something about them induces great delight in Mary, and her high-pitched, girlish laughter often accompanies these spectacles. Understandably, these experiences often leave the uninitiated somewhat uneasy. For the inured, it's just another day with Mary.

Kitchen staff report hearing mysterious knocks from inside the walk-in freezer. When the door is flung open, all that greets their disbelieving eyes is row upon row of frozen goods. In the kitchen itself, water taps turn themselves on. When cooks turn them off, they stubbornly open once again, gushing streams of water. They only stop when staff tells Mary that it's enough. Thoroughly chastised, Mary's unseen hands then turn the taps off. Bartenders often come in for their first shift of the day to find margarita glasses they hung the night before lined up on the bar in a neat little row. During closing, Mary, desirous of company, will become petulant and toss kitchen pans and cookware to the floor in a pout. "She gets bored like any little kid and wants someone to play with," Darden told Henion. To put the spirit at ease, waiters, waitresses, cooks and other staff now make sure to bid Mary goodnight before they leave. It seems to go a long way toward reassuring the child.

Henion relates a bizarre experience waitress Molly Cooper had with Mary. When she first began working at Tijuana Fats, Cooper was unfamiliar with the spirit, and one day she bent down to examine the footprints on the hearth. Another waitress came upon her and warned her to stop. That night and for a few nights after, Cooper found her sleep haunted by a recurring dream in which Mary tried to possess her body. When Cooper revealed her anguish to another waitress, she gave her a simple though odd piece of advice. "Say goodnight to Mary before you leave," the waitress said. Cooper did, and ever since has not experienced the dream.

Few individuals can actually count themselves among what Darden refers to as "Mary's chosen": the lucky people who've actually glimpsed the spirit herself. Not surprisingly, many children have seen Mary and even held conversations with her. Their descriptions have proven uniform and sturdy. She's painted as a young girl, no older than eight and no younger than four, who is blessed with a head of strawberry blonde tresses and garbed in a petticoat. "She likes having people to play with," Darden told Henion.

When Halloween rolls around, Mary is thrust into the spotlight, complete with her own party and a roster of admirers who gather to gaze, once again, upon her footsteps in the hearth. Mary would surely be grateful for the company and the attention. Tijuana Fats diners, for their part, are treated to a dining experience quite unlike any other.

East Hall at Appalachian State University

For the students who live in Appalachian State University's East Hall in Boone, North Carolina, life can sometimes be a little bit unnerving. Never mind the essays, the exams, the all-night cram sessions and the bland cafeteria food, East Hall residents also have to contend with the presence of a particularly mischievous and impish spirit fond of frightening the uninitiated with her laughter and her pranks.

The identity of East Hall's resident ghost is unknown. As it is with many university hauntings, her origins are questionable and fantastic, rooted more in lore than in actual fact. Regardless, the most commonly accepted explanation is that years ago, a female student, disconsolate over her studies, or her boyfriend or her family (take your pick—each is as valid as the next), decided that she'd had enough of life. Late one evening, she entered the girls' bathroom in the East Hall basement and hanged herself. Given the gruesome nature of her death and the pitched aura of emotions surely involved in the undertaking, the girl's spirit remained tethered to this corporeal plane, destined to roam the halls of East Hall in perpetuity. While her origins may be endlessly debated, few would argue that East Hall isn't haunted, for it most assuredly is. Countless students have encountered the spirit; their accounts are often similar in nature.

As ever, the ghost is fond of turning lights on and off, brushing unseen but not unfelt by people walking down the halls and whispering in otherwise empty rooms. Megan

Arsenault (a pseudonym), who graduated from the university's Interdisciplinary Studies Department, still remembers her encounters with the East Hall ghost as if they occurred yesterday.

"Everything about that basement in the East Hall creeped me out," she recalls. "I'd go into a classroom or the bathroom and just feel…weird. There was this real eerie, creepy sensation about the place. Sometimes, I'd just shudder." She still remembers the time she arrived early for an evening lecture. The hall was deserted and as she walked, her footsteps echoing along the linoleum flooring, she heard something that stopped her dead in her tracks. "I heard a voice," she says. "It was really breathy and low, just barely a whisper. But I heard it as clear as day." Megan cocked her head, trying to determine its source, but couldn't. "It seemed to be coming at me in stereo surround sound," she says. Perturbed, she went into the bathroom to throw cold water on her face. "I thought that I was just really tired and needed to wake up," she explains. While in the bathroom, Megan heard something else: the slap of a heel against the linoleum in the hall.

"At first," she continues, "I thought it was people coming to class." Yet, when Megan opened the door, she found herself staring down an empty hallway, the footsteps still resounding in her ears. "I was completely freaked out," she says. "Because then I knew, too, that I'd definitely heard the voice." Other students (living, breathing ones) eventually did arrive and Megan spotted her friends among them. Hurriedly, she related her story and learned, to her great relief, that she was not the only one to have experienced the strange phenomena. She even heard about how one of her friends had actually seen an apparition. "She described it as a shadow that flitted into her field of vision for just a second," she says. "Then, it was gone." Megan recalls that she did, in time, adapt to the presence of East Hall's ghost but admits that she still found using the downstairs bathroom creepy.

East Hall's ghost seems particularly fond of the bathroom. In an interview with Amy Burnette of *The Appalachian Online*, the university's online campus newspaper, Renee A. Richards, an East Hall Resident Assistant, described how she "hears and feels a presence every time she's in the restroom alone."

"Every time I go into the restroom," Richards told Burnette, "I always hear the door directly beside me lock and then unlock. It doesn't matter which stall I'm in, I'll always hear it. Whenever I go out of the stall to look, no one is ever around. It only happens when I'm by myself. If there're other people in the restroom, then it won't happen."

Burnette also detailed the experiences of freshman Elena Borisoff, who encountered East Hall's spirited presence almost immediately after moving in. She had just finished showering and, while walking back to her dorm room, felt "some sort of presence, like someone was walking behind [her]." Elena stopped and looked around, but saw nobody there. Shrugging it off, she continued to her bedroom, shut the door and opened her closet. As she sorted out what she was going to wear, Elena heard a voice, which she attributes to a young girl, whisper to her. The voice said, "Look at me. Look through the peephole." Elena did but when she looked through the fisheye lens, she saw nothing but the distorted vision of an empty hallway. To be sure, it was a unique initiation to East Hall life, one to which Cora Schultz can certainly relate.

One night, Schultz was hard at work, cramming for an exam. She rubbed her eyes, threw her pen down and decided to take a break. Stretching her back, Cora looked at her clock. It was three in the morning. The dorm was dark and quiet. She grabbed a bowl of instant noodles and went to the lounge to make herself a quick snack. As she waited for the microwave to finish its work, she heard what sounded like footsteps approaching from the stairwell. She then heard the stairwell door slam shut. Curious to see who it was, Cora opened the door and peered out from the lounge. She looked at the stairwell door and then down the hallway. With a frown, she realized that there was nobody there, but she was positive that she had heard footsteps. It wasn't until later that she learned that East Hall was haunted. "Suddenly," she says, "everything made sense. All the strange things that I'd experienced over the semester."

Cora continues, "One time, I was alone in my room, getting ready to go out, when someone began jiggling my doorknob. I could see someone trying to turn it." Cora even called out a couple of times for whoever it was to just come in. When the door remained shut and the doorknob continued to jiggle, she threw down her comb and flung open the door. "There was nobody there," she says. When she closed the door, the jiggling resumed, more determined and persistent than ever. "I looked through the peephole," she remembers. "But there was nobody there. I swear, I could hear someone laughing at me. As if the ghost was watching me and just having a grand ol' time." When she left her room to investigate further, the laughter only increased. As Cora approached the bathroom, it got louder and louder. Standing outside the bathroom door, Cora was convinced that the laughter was coming from that room yet when she opened the door, she found herself standing in an empty restroom. Then the laughter stopped. "I even looked under the stall doors," she says. "But I didn't see anything or anyone. It was so bizarre."

With so many hauntings all over East Hall, one must assume that the resident spirit is either incredibly active or not completely alone. Caroline Cox would believe it's the latter. In an interview with Burnette, Cox described one eerie morning. "It was about 5:30 AM and I was in the restroom," Cox, a freshman, told Burnette. "I looked around like my mom and dad always told me to do, you know, to make sure no one was there. I came out of the stall and looked to my right and saw something. I had to look again to make sure I was really seeing something, and there was a man sitting in the shower stall. He was sitting straight up, his arms crossed in his lap and was staring straight at me."

The man looked as if he were in his late 30s, and he sat completely still with his head "cocked to the right" and just stared at the freshman. Who is this other ghost? No one knows his identity, though according to legend his name might just be Scratch, a moniker bequeathed years ago by those most familiar with him. Whether or not he works in concert with the anonymous female spirit of East Hall is unknown, but for the students of Appalachian State University, a spirited life in the dormitory takes on a different meaning altogether.

Lees-McRae College

Nestled in the bosom of the mountains of western North Carolina is the little community of Banner Elk, home to Lees-McRae College. Banner Elk was first settled in 1850 and, as a new century dawned, the Presbyterian Church firmly established itself within the community. In 1895, a young student from Union Theological Seminary was sent to organize a church. Four years later, disturbed by the distinct lack of education offered by the district schools, the young reverend, Edgar Tufts, took it upon himself to educate a small group of the community's youth. Such are the origins of Lees-McRae College, named for Elizabeth A. McRae, a South Carolinian well known for her devotion to teaching, and S.P. Lees of Kentucky, a generous benefactor. The institute became coeducational in 1927 and formally became Lees-McRae College in 1931. Over the last century, people have come and gone through Lees-McRae, but not surprisingly, there is one who has never been quite willing to leave. Her name is Emily, and she is a beloved piece of Lees-McRae lore. Appropriately enough, her tombstone near the Banner Elk Presbyterian Church allegedly bears the following epitaph: *She is not dead, but sleeping.*

In life, Emily had been known as Miss Emily Draughn. How she met her death is a matter up for debate. Some believe Emily was a young girl who, at the tender age of 12, lost her life to tuberculosis in the 1930s. She succumbed to the disease in her bed at what was once Grace Memorial Hospital. Other say that Emily was a resident of the hospital's psychiatric ward and that she leapt to her death from a fourth floor window. Today, the four-story structure that squats just off the campus entrance is formally known as Tate Dormitory, and is informally known as Emily's home. She has a reputation as a positive and innocent spirit, though undeniably mischievous and still blessed with the impishness of youth.

Scott Nicholson, a writer for the *Watauga Democrat*, visited the Lees-McRae campus in the fall of 2004 to see for himself if the stories about Emily were true. For Tiffany Solesbee, then a sophomore living at Tate, Emily's presence was a fact. She was often on the end of Emily's pranks and she recalled to Nicholson how the television in her dorm room was prone to turning itself on.

Serena Wright, then a junior, could relate. Her television also turned itself on and off. "It does that until I tell her to stop," Wright told Nicholson. Wright became accustomed to Emily and claimed, "She's not scary. She's a good ghost." Wright also went on to describe the experiences of one of her friends living on the first floor. Her friend found peace and quiet in her room particularly elusive, disrupted constantly by her phone, which would ring on the hour every hour. Each and every time that she answered, the line was dead.

One girl reported that when she returned to her dorm room following the Christmas break, she was shocked to discover that everything in her room had been rearranged and that someone had scribbled on the wall. Others have heard the ubiquitous phantom footsteps in deserted hallways and even caught a glimpse of a shadowy shape floating past open doorways. Though Emily is most often associated with the Tate Dormitory, she sometimes does stray from familiar ground and has been seen and felt in the Carson Library.

There, librarians and students alike have watched empty elevators moving between floors all by themselves, and the building is prone to experiencing mysterious power surges that Sherry Johnson, who worked in the periodical section, attributes to Emily's presence. She also holds Emily responsible for the events that took place one day in the Stirling Room, the locked site of the library's Appalachian collection and other exhibits.

"Two students went to do research last year," she told Nicholson. "One said that she didn't believe in Emily." The proclamation seemed to pique Emily and, almost immediately, the two started hearing noises that sounded like "old radiator pipes heating up." As the two students worked, the noise increased in volume. Finally, the skeptical girl fled the room, swearing never to return. Oddly enough, people outside the room heard nothing unusual. On another occasion, a work-study student was shelving books alone in the Stirling Room. At least, he thought he was alone. As he worked, his gaze fell upon a woman clad in a black dress. In her hands, she held a bouquet of flowers. The student approached her and firmly told her that she would have to leave because the room was restricted. She promptly vanished before his very eyes.

"When things disappear off my desk," said Ramona Hayes, a library employee, "I always blame Emily." When staffers complain to maintenance about how the furnace isn't working, their concerns are dismissed with a laugh. "Hey, those cold spots are Emily's fault," maintenance workers will say, "not ours." Emily is nothing, it seems, if not a convenient scapegoat.

While there are skeptics who dismiss the stories about Emily with a derisive laugh, those who do believe have embraced her. Childish pranks and scapegoating aside, all use the warmest of adjectives to describe the impish spirit who has captured a permanent place in Lees-McRae folklore. Hearing these stories, it's not hard to imagine that her epitaph is all too true. It really does seem as if Emily isn't dead and that she's only sleeping.

Brunswick Inn

Overlooking the Cape Fear River and offering panoramic vistas of Bald Head Island is the Southport institution known as the Brunswick Inn. Blessed by geography and climate, the Brunswick Inn, a modest building of the Federal style, is a quaint hideaway, the sort of restful place that harkens back to a simpler and peaceful time. The building boasts original heart pine floors, plaster ceiling moldings, louvered cathedral-shaped pocket doors and nine working fireplaces—all elements first put in place in the early 19th century when the building was first constructed.

Originally constructed as the summer home of Benjamin Smith, founder of Smithville (today's Southport) and the 10th governor of North Carolina, the home overlooked the mouths of the Cape Fear River, the Intracoastal Waterway and the Atlantic Ocean. In 1856, its top two floors were rebuilt by Thomas Meares, the owner of the Orton Plantation. Having served as a tavern and a boarding house, the Brunswick Inn's original splendor had been abraded over the years. Several years ago, Jim and Judy Clary bought the building, set to restoring its grandeur and reopened the Brunswick Inn as a bed and breakfast. Watching it all has been longtime Brunswick Inn resident Antonio Caselleta, a harpist who perished in 1882 and who has since made the inn his home.

Caselleta had come to Southport by way of New York City, where he had left his Italian family behind in the hopes of earning his fortunes as a riverboat and hotel musician. With two friends and his harp in tow, Caselleta bid goodbye to the cruel winters of the American Northeast and happily sailed south, regaling passengers with the melodious combination of the harp, cello and mandolin. Lacking money, the Caselleta trio disembarked in North Carolina and eventually worked their way down the Atlantic coast from Wilmington to the little seaside town of Southport.

Really just a village of Victorian homes, antique stores and restaurants, Southport possessed the peaceful splendor that had made the Brunswick Inn, overlooking the Cape Fear River, a beloved spot for summering North Carolinians. Summertime galas were common, and as Caselleta watched the tourists come and go, he decided to make the innkeeper an offer. In exchange for temporary shelter, the trio would give concerts and offer a helping hand around the inn. The audition was all the innkeeper needed to hear. The agreement was struck and soon, Caselleta and his friends were entertaining guests at the Brunswick Inn. So popular did they become that they were soon hired to perform for private recitals throughout the county and were earning enough to move from the Brunswick Inn into a well-appointed home of their own. They insinuated themselves within the fabric of the Southport community and for a brief time, life for the harpist was good. But then came the dawning of a tragic day.

One sunny afternoon, Caselleta and his friends were casting about for something to do. They had worked hard that week and were seeking some form of relaxation to salve their tired souls. They had often spoken of taking a ship and sailing toward Bald Head Island, and this day seemed like the perfect day. The waters were calm, shimmering beneath the sun like a rippling mirror. But they made one grave error. None of them were sailors and none had any experience whatsoever with the craft. Recklessly, they rented a small boat and set off, with much gumption but little else.

They were still over half the distance away from Bald Head Island when their craft capsized. The three musicians were cast from the vessel but while the cellist and mandolinist were thrown clear, Caselleta dashed his head against the prow of the boat. The blow rendered him unconscious and he drowned before his friends were able to rescue him. Days later, Caselleta was laid to rest at Smithville Burial Ground.

The night of the funeral, Caselleta and his friends had been scheduled to perform at the Brunswick Inn and, while no one would have faulted the surviving two for canceling, they gamely chose not to, believing that they could best honor their fallen friend's life by playing. When they took to the stage that night, they set up Caselleta's harp between them. Everyone in the room watched the performance stunned and transfixed. Though Caselleta rested quietly beneath the ground, his spirit was clearly in the room that night. The sweet lilting music of his harp soared through the air and it was as if he were in the room, his fingers plucking the strings with the greatest of ease.

Since that time, Caselleta's spirit has made itself welcome at the Brunswick Inn as an eternal guest. Many have heard his harp playing quietly through the halls. Nathan Benedict, who asked not to be identified by his real name, is just such an individual.

He stayed at the inn not too long ago and was quite eager to share his account. While Benedict's first night at the inn was spirit free, the next was decidedly not. "I'd gone to sleep pretty early. I'd packed my bags and was going to get an early start on the day," Benedict recalls, "and at about two in the morning, I just suddenly woke up." Footsteps had roused him from slumber and he sat straight up in his bed, peering into the darkness. He saw nothing, but could still hear the footsteps. "They were right in the room," Benedict says. "Someone was definitely in that room with me." Benedict turned on the light, but everything was as it should have been. He called out, but was greeted with silence. The footsteps padded away toward the door. Benedict assumed he must have imagined it all and quickly drifted back to sleep.

The following morning, Benedict was surprised to find his room door slightly ajar. "I'm positive it was locked," Benedict avers, "and it was definitely shut when I went back to sleep." When Benedict returned home later that evening, he was surprised to discover that his clothes, which he had neatly packed the day before, were all ruffled and tangled. "It was as if someone had gone through [my bag] after I'd packed," Benedict describes. "It was really freaky." Only later, when Benedict began some minor research into the Brunswick Inn, did he learn about its ghostly guest. "It had to be Tony," Benedict states firmly. "There's just no other explanation." While he doesn't regret having had a run-in with the specter, he wishes that he'd heard the music of the harp instead. "I hate ironing," he says. "And I spent the next couple of hours after I got back doing just that. All my clothes were wrinkled. I'm not a huge fan of harp music, but yeah, it'd have been a little more considerate."

Antonio Caselleta, the Italian immigrant who dreamt of making his mark as a musician, has done exactly that. His legacy has had a longevity far outstripping that of his brief and ultimately tragic existence, though one imagines that he must be quite content to remain at the Brunswick Inn. Even death has not been able to keep him from his love for the harp.

5
Tragedies and Mysteries

The Devil's Tramping Ground

In this age of science and reason, when almost everything has a plausible explanation grounded in logical and rational conclusions, it's not difficult to understand why some people place little faith in a deity and doubt the existence of true evil. Science has little room for God and the Devil. But the God-fearing folk of Siler City, North Carolina, know better. To the doubters and atheists, they might say, "Take a trip to the Devil's Tramping Ground and let your faith be restored."

The legend of the Devil's Tramping Ground has fascinated North Carolinians and others for centuries. It is one of the state's most persistent and beloved tales, and it's not hard to see why. The story is a fantastical one and has been passed down for generations. It's been told, and retold, and it always seems to have a place reserved in the columns and broadcasts of local media at Halloween. If the story is true, then the Devil's Tramping Ground is proof positive of the Devil's very existence. If not, then it's still a very good story that has become a colorful chapter in North Carolina folklore.

In the late 18th century, as settlers tamed the remaining wilds of North Carolina, they found something utterly unsettling within the woods of Chatham County, just 10 miles from what would eventually become Siler City. There, in the wilderness, settlers came across a well-worn circular path, 40 feet in diameter, surrounding a space in which absolutely nothing grew. Pines, oaks and brush surrounded the circle but within it, not even the smallest stem of a hardy weed could be found. Stranger still, horses whinnied and reared up any time they came close to the path and refused to advance

The Devil's Tramping Ground is a well-worn circular path inside which nothing grows.

any farther. Dogs, yipping loudly, scurried away as quickly as they could with their tails pressed firmly between their legs. To the settlers, the path was wholly unnatural. Nature just didn't create perfect circles in the middle of nowhere. It was a tantalizing mystery and, for a short while, it seemed to some of the settlers that they had solved it.

They surmised that the circle was a popular meeting ground for roaming bands of the dark-skinned Native people who populated the continent. Inside the circle these tribes would have lush feasts and wild celebrations marked by countless pairs of feet pounding the ground in time to the ominous beats of a drum. This strange, frenzied dance, which many of them had observed firsthand in other parts of Chatham County, could easily have pounded out a barren patch in the woods.

But the explanation didn't sit well with the more observant settlers. If dancing was the cause, why then, they asked, did the circle arouse such primal fear in their horses and dogs? Why did anything that they put on the path, such as a stone or a large branch, mysteriously disappear? How could the ground magically clean itself of all debris? To them, there was only one reasonable explanation and it had nothing to do with the natives. In fact, they pointed out, the Native American tribes avoided the area altogether. The settlers concluded that barren circle in which nothing grew was the tramping ground of the Devil himself. "He comes at night," they whispered to one another. "He comes to this ground to plot our destruction. He walks in that circle, and he's poisoned the land, burning it up like Hell itself." To many of the locals, this explanation made perfect sense.

There were skeptics, of course, and a few of them set out to spend the night at the Devil's Tramping Ground, determined to disprove the theory. Not one of them made it through the night. Each eventually fled from the circle, his blanket wrapped tightly around his body and his eyes wildly declaring he had seen enough and couldn't bear to see more. Each returned a true believer.

As the years passed and Chatham County's original settlers gave way to their descendants, the one constant remained the Devil's Tramping Ground, always fascinating and provoking the curious. Other explanations were offered as the 19th century gave way to the 20th. Perhaps it had been the location of a grinding mill, and the horses that circled around to turn the mill and grind the cane had pounded out the circle with their hooves. Opponents argued that if this were the case, why hadn't nature reclaimed the land? Why did it remain barren while other similar spots did not?

In the 1950s, with UFO mania reaching a fevered pitch, some people speculated that the circle was the landing site for extraterrestrials, or that perhaps it was one of the oldest examples of alleged alien activity: the crop circle. Others returned once more to the settlers' original explanation and suggested that perhaps it was the work of Indian rituals. However, Native Americans had been driven from Chatham County long ago, so why wouldn't vegetation have sprung up somewhere in the cursed circle since then? But for all the different opinions, it's the one citing the work of Lucifer, or Satan or Beezlebub or whatever you call him, that has proven the sturdiest.

Nancy Roberts, in her collection *North Carolina Ghosts and Legends*, relates a story told by a reverend in the 1950s, in which a group of young men from Bennett dared one of their own to spend the night in the circle. Boldly, he accepted the challenge. But at about 11:30 in the evening, as the reverend was driving home from his brother's house, "he passed a blanketed figure heading toward town as fast as his legs could carry him." The young man said nothing about aliens or UFOs; he just said that he felt some terrible evil in the air and could stand it no longer.

As Roberts explains, the story grew so popular and became so firmly entrenched within the public imagination that in the 1950s, scientists and the state began taking an active interest in the reported phenomenon.

Tests were conducted on the soil, and one revealed an abnormally high level of salt while another revealed that the earth was altogether sterile. Though the former appeared to have offered a reasonable explanation for the absence of plant life, the test didn't explain how the salt could be concentrated in such a perfect circle. The latter affirmed the violation of natural laws. How could soil be sterile when, mere yards away, trees and brush flourished? More importantly, no one could explain how the ground remained clear of all debris. Anything placed on the ground simply vanished. It had to be the prince of darkness himself, clearing the land with his feet as he paced around.

Recently, however, it seems as if the Lord of the Underworld might have better things to do with his nights than tramp around a patch of earth in Chatham County. In early December 2001, a group of paranormal investigators from Metrolina Paranormal Research drove to Siler City. They took Highway 421 south and then headed down Route 902. From there, it was a short drive to a gravel parking lot and a short walk down a small, well-traveled path to the infamous Devil's Tramping Ground.

The group had brought an array of tools designed to scientifically determine whether or not there was anything strange about the area. They had cameras, both digital and film, Electromagnetic Field (EMF) detectors and a relatively low-tech measuring tape. They arrived 1:30 PM. What they found bore little resemblance to the stories that they had heard. There was indeed a clearing, but its diameter spanned not the legendary 40 feet but a rather paltry and disappointing 14 feet. It was barren, but the investigators quickly decided that it had less to do with the Master of All Evil than with the one-inch layer of ash that covered the earth. The ash, it was clear, had come from the countless campfires that bored teenagers, lured by the story of the Devil's Tramping Ground, had set. Evidence of their late-night carousals was all around.

Beer cans, broken glass and cigarette butts abounded, and as the investigators quipped, "It could be said that if Satan himself is a frequent visitor to this location, then it appears his preferred beer is Budweiser and that he smokes Marlboro cigarettes." Comparing the circle to photographs taken of it in the 1950s, Metrolina Paranormal Research concluded that plant growth had clearly taken place inside what might have once been a 40-foot circle. Exploring further, they found a system of well-worn trails radiating from the ground like spokes on a wheel. Two of the trails led to more campfire sites and, not surprisingly, more beer cans and litter. In the end, the researchers concluded that the area was far from the 40-foot perfect circle of barren earth that they'd expected, and that there was no sign of strange or unusual activity. Though there were certainly barren patches in the Devil's Tramping Ground, they attributed the lack of vegetation to the high volume of foot traffic and ash. As for the legend of the Devil's Tramping Ground, they determined that it was nothing but a "self-perpetuating myth."

Though many would disagree with Metrolina Paranormal Research, the group is not alone in its conclusions. Kurt Blatter, a paranormal enthusiast, has visited the site a number of times and each time comes away convinced only that "the place is a popular place for kids to party. The scariest thing I ever saw was a green and moldy sandwich. I had to keep my dog from eating it." Unlike the settlers' dogs,

Blatter's dog has never seemed fearful of the Devil's Tramping Ground, running quite happily from one end to another, sniffing and rooting through the earth. The two of them even spent the night in a tent there not too long ago. "I didn't see anything strange, I didn't hear anything strange and I certainly didn't feel anything strange," Blatter recalls. Jim Hall, co-director of Haunted North Carolina Paranormal Research and Investigations, is equally blunt. "I've been out there," he says with a laugh, "and it is a bare patch in the wood. But it's so cluttered with litter and beer cans and cigarette butts—the devil is really slacking off on the job. He's not taking stuff out like he's supposed to be." Maybe the devil is taking some time off. Maybe, and this idea may be particularly frightening, he feels as if he doesn't have as much to do. Perhaps the politicians and corporations have done enough. Because, despite the conclusions of Metrolina Paranormal Research, Haunted North Carolina Paranormal Research and Investigations and one Kurt Blatter, Roxie Zuban still believes.

As a little girl growing up in nearby Siler City, Roxie heard about the Devil's Tramping Ground and wished to see it for herself. Her parents, however, never seemed to take much interest in the site, and it wasn't until one of her friends finally got a driver's license that she was finally able to realize her dream. The place wasn't hard to find. Handmade signs abounded along the dirt road, offering directions and reassurances that they were close. Roxie and her friends parked their car and, after an unpleasant hike through 40 yards of thorns, poison ivy and thick brush, they reached the area.

According to Roxie, "It was kind of disappointing to look at for the first time. It's just a bare circle with nothing growing in it. And in the day, everything seemed perfectly normal." It wasn't until the sun set that things started feeling a little off.

Roxie and her friends made numerous attempts to spend the night but have never succeeded. "Each time, we'd hear something strange," she laments, "and we'd always end up feeling terrified with a really strong sense of dread and evil in our stomachs." They have usually ended up fleeing to the safety of their car and the open road. Roxie also firmly states that items placed along the path will disappear. Over the years, she and her friends have deposited all kinds of objects, including toys, trinkets and, most bizarre of all, a huge weight borrowed from a parent's gym.

"The thing weighed over 100 pounds," Roxie says. "And we dragged the damn thing through the woods and left it there on the ground." When Roxie and her friends returned later, the plate was nowhere to be found. "I could understand the toys and stuff going missing. I mean, a lot of people hang out there," Roxie explains. "But who in their right mind would go to the trouble of lugging the stupid weight out of there? It doesn't make sense." One might reason that if they made the effort to bring it out there, it wouldn't be completely unreasonable to think that someone else might make the effort to spirit it away. Roxie dismisses the suggestion with a laugh. "People don't go out there to take things away," she says. "They go there to party, to drink. Something else took that plate away. The same thing that always scared us away. You've got to be there to believe it. I'm a level-headed girl and the fear I've felt there—it's totally real. You can't deny it. There's an evil in that place, I'm sure of it."

Regardless of the circle's origins, it has provided a time-honored story, truly a part of North Carolina folklore. It seems clear that there will always be believers and doubters, and there will always be an eager audience for a good story. Say what you will, but the Devil's Tramping Ground is relentlessly fascinating, touching something primitive and ancient within us all.

Brown Mountain Lights

The Northern and Southern Lights, Aurora Borealis and Aurora Australis, are tendrils of ethereal light that flicker across the star-lit sky in shades of blues, greens and reds. The phenomena are most intense near the North and South Poles but also occur in other parts of the Northern and Southern Hemispheres. Those living in the continental United States may never witness these brilliant spectacles, but the people of Burke County, North Carolina are often treated to their own spectacular light show radiating from the foothills of the Blue Ridge, atop the long, low Brown Mountain.

The lights have been seen for centuries. They move up and down across the night sky, illuminated orbs of blue and red that rise thick and fast above the horizon. There are many varied explanations for the eerie lights. Some theories are rooted in science, while others use hypotheses less empirical but no less persuasive. Are the Brown Mountain Lights evidence of an underground alien base? Are the lights the spirit of a corpse found long ago at the foot of the mountain? Whatever their origins, these lights have held sway over the imaginations of all those who've gazed upon them. So pervasive was the phenomenon that even the United States Geological Survey attempted to unlock its mysteries. But those who have attempted to do so have learned that the Brown Mountain Lights do not yield the answers to its riddle so easily.

The Cherokee looked upon the lights with a religious reverence. Gathered upon the hills around Brown Mountain, the Cherokee would recount to their collected youth the story of a great battle fought in the year 1200. When the battle had come to its end, the air was thick and ferric, heavy with the scent of blood and the incessant buzzing of flies. Families walked about, torches in hand, searching for loved ones. The flies scattered ahead of them and their buzzing gave way to wails of anger and loss. The devastation was almost too much to bear. The dead were wrapped in their burial shrouds and interred.

The tribe and the land were scarred. Even after the rain had washed away the blood, the field still echoed with the whispers of the dead. The eerie lights rose above the ridge of the Brown Mountain, moving back and forth across the horizon. Today's Cherokee cannot help but remember their ancestors when they look upon the lights. Cherokee lore tells that the lights are lingering remnants of the spirits of the Indian maidens who walked the fields in search of their loved ones.

The earliest European settlers shared the Cherokees' belief, but it wasn't long before the rational minds of these foreigners rejected the idea of the paranormal in favor of more quantifiable evidence. In 1771, German engineer Gerard William de Brahm, his professional interest piqued by the breathless accounts he'd heard of the lights, set out for Wiseman's View on Linville Mountain, the perfect vantage point from which to observe the phenomenon. Applying his knowledge of gas and combustion, de Brahm concluded that the mountains were spewing gaseous vapors that were carried along the wind. When one breeze met another, the resulting friction caused the vapors to ignite, resulting in the bursts of light along the ridge. His theory was eventually disproven. No nitrous vapors, as he called them, were escaping from the earth. By the early 20th century, the local phenomenon had attracted enough national attention to merit a study by the U.S. Geological Survey.

The organization's scientists came to North Carolina in 1913, armed with the latest in monitoring equipment and a determination to solve the mystery. After a few days of surveying and measuring, they decided that the Brown Mountain Lights were little more than the distortion of something very common and ordinary. The only unusual things at work here, they claimed, were some of the laws of physics. The lights were nothing more than locomotive headlights approaching from the Catawba Valley to the south. However, the scientists had ignored one little but highly significant detail. The Cherokee had seen the lights long before the iron horse ever came to North Carolina. Three years later, a flood roared through the Catawba Valley, sweeping the railroad bridges away. Repairs took weeks. All trains through the valley were suspended. Strangely enough, the Brown Mountain Lights continued to flicker.

A scientist with the U.S. Weather Bureau was also asked to investigate the lights. Dr. Humphries was not surprised by the spectacle. He immediately thought of other light-related phenomena such as St. Elmo's Fire and the Andes Lights of South America. The former is a scientifically accepted occurrence and has been described by Julius Caesar, William Shakespeare and Herman Melville. The lights are usually seen around projections, say a chimney or a church spire, before or after thunderstorm. The bright spheres of light are the result of atoms being stripped of their electrons. Regardless, Dr. Humphries could not explain why the Brown

Mountain Lights could be seen on days when the skies were clear and when there had been no thunderstorms.

By the 1960s, a small population believed that it had uncovered the roots of the Brown Mountain Lights. Ralph Lael, a shop owner who worked near the area, claimed that aliens had abducted him 1962. He believed that the lights were from the aliens' UFOs. According to Lael, the ridge is a landing pad for extraterrestrial visitors, and the mountains themselves may hide an underground alien base. Lael believed aliens had come seeking information about earth life before returning to their unknown origins, and he claimed to be the victim of numerous abductions. He also stated that during one of his trips aboard a UFO, he was able to obtain what he called an "alien mummy," a figure standing just 3 to 4 feet high. Its physiology indicated that it walked upright and it had four limbs just like humans, but there the similarities ended. Its face was something from a dream, with features undeniably foreign in origin.

For years, Lael displayed the figure in a glass coffin in his Outer Space Rock Shop Museum on Highway 181 outside Morganton. He dismissed all other explanations, suggesting that all theories save his were just smoke screens and signs of a vast conspiracy to keep the existence of extraterrestrial life a secret. Conspiracy theorists who rallied around Lael during his lifetime also rallied around the former congressional candidate in death. They found it suspicious that after Lael's death, the alien mummy he had displayed so proudly disappeared under mysterious circumstances.

No one can offer a satisfactory explanation for the Brown Mountain Lights. Tragedy lies at the core of most of these theories, like in the story of the dedicated slave who wandered out into the mountains to search for his master. The slave knew the land well and took with him only some provisions and a lamp to light his way. His master knew the land well too, and survival in the wilderness had been part of his training when he joined the Confederate Army. When neither master nor slave returned, people wondered what had happened on the mountain. The two bodies were never found, but the lights might very well be the lamps of the phantom master and slave still trying to find a way home.

Dromgoole's Rock

Just a short remove west of of the basketball-crazy University of North Carolina's campus at Chapel Hill sits Dromgoole's Rock. It's an idyllic place and ideal for young lovers: quiet, wooded and set atop a cliff affording a vista of the surrounding landscape. It is also a tragic place that bears visible scars of its past. According to local legend, the body of Peter Dromgoole lies beneath the stone. His spirit is said to haunt the grounds and his blood has stained the rock for years, resisting all manner of wind and rain.

In 1833, a young Virginian named Peter Dromgoole arrived at Chapel Hill to study at the University of North Carolina. A few months later, he met a local young girl known today simply as Fanny. As the trees and flowers bloomed around them, bringing spectacular color and life to the campus, so grew their love. They met often in secret, stealing away to their favorite meeting place: a large, flat rock near the cliff, beneath the shadows of Gimghoul Castle on Piney Prospect. Fanny usually arrived first and, as she waited, she luxuriated in the sunlight that shimmered through the canopy of leaves fluttering above. It wasn't long before she glimpsed Peter's long, lanky silhouette loping down the winding trail leading him directly to her embrace. And so it was that these two lovers spent their days, dappled by the sun and basking in the glow of their affection. Happiness was theirs and they dreamt of a rosy future. The fates, unfortunately, conspired to deny them.

Fanny waited one day on the large, flat rock, but Peter was late. It wasn't a surprise. He always was. Except on this day

The scenic University of North Carolina at Chapel Hill

and the next, and the one following that, he never showed. Spring gave way to summer, and the green leaves of her canopy succumbed to the oranges, yellows and reds of fall, but he still didn't show. All the while, the rock upon which Fanny sat slowly became stained with spots of rusty brown. She had noticed the marks but never suspected that they had anything to do with Peter's unexpected disappearance.

Desperate, she finally contacted Peter's family and learned from his tearful mother and father that they hadn't the faintest clue as to where their child might have gone. All they had left of him was a mysterious letter that had arrived not long after his disappearance. Cryptically, Peter had written that despite the best of his intentions, he would probably bring great sadness to them, and that in all likelihood they would never hear from or see him again. His dormitory room closet at Chapel Hill was still full of the clothes he had originally packed with him, and his trunk squatted empty at the foot of his bed. If he had gone somewhere, he was surely traveling light.

Fanny cried often, returning with diminishing hope to the rock, where sometimes the lengthening shadows of twilight would fool her into thinking that her Peter had returned. When she realized it was only an illusion, she would throw herself against the rock, her tears mingling with the rusty brown stain. She died never knowing what had happened to Peter Dromgoole. Some say she died of a broken heart that time never fully healed.

Sixty years later, in the late 19th century, Peter's mysterious disappearance was finally explained. As he lay fading on his deathbed, a man who had once been a student at the University of North Carolina related the tragic tale of Peter Dromgoole and his beloved Fanny.

Though Peter had won Fanny's affections, she had had other persistent and devoted admirers. Unfortunately, among them was a close friend of Peter's. As it is so often with romantic rivals, their friendship became strained and then quickly cooled. Peter made every effort to avoid his old friend, though the friend seemed to take particular delight in seeking Peter out and goading him at every opportunity. One afternoon, Peter and his rival passed one another on campus; the latter shoved Peter with his shoulder with such force that Peter's hat was knocked from his head. A heated argument followed and curses and epithets flew through the air thick and fast. The rival, incensed, issued a challenge to Peter: a duel, with pistols, at 10 paces. Enraged, Peter accepted.

North Carolina had outlawed dueling in 1802 although, by all accounts, it was still a proper and accepted means for gentlemen to settle a dispute. North Carolinians just had to go to South Carolina or Tennessee to do it, or do it in secret. Peter and his rival laid out their furtive plans. The two would meet at midnight with their chosen seconds; the location would be the cliff on which Peter had spent many an after-noon with his beloved Fanny.

Peter was confident; his aim was sharp, his shooting hand steady. But on that particular night, skill hardly mattered. A day of light rain had given way to a thick fog that clung tena-ciously to the ground; trees and figures were little more than murky silhouettes—ghosts in the mists. Peter and his friend-turned-enemy approached each other and then, with their backs to one another, began walking the appointed 10 paces. Seconds later, two shots rang out almost simultaneously. In the gloom, no one could be sure exactly what had happened.

But then, Peter's groans issued forth from the fog and his second ran to where he lay. His white shirt was now a brilliant shade of crimson and as Peter lay with his head cradled in the shaking hands of his second, he breathed his last breath and was still. It was an agonizing moment and in a panic everyone there decided that they had only one option: hide the evi-dence. No one must ever know what had happened.

They dragged Peter's body from the cliff and up toward a huge rock. With their bare hands, they began digging into the loamy soil, burrowing out a pitiful shallow grave. With bloodied knuckles and fingers, they lowered Peter into the ground then, as quickly as they could, rolled the rock onto the shallow grave, burying him in the darkness. The group left that night only after swearing a solemn vow never to speak again of what had taken place on the cliff.

Years later, Dromgoole's Rock still tells the story of Peter and Fanny. The rock bears the reddish stains that many people believe signify Peter's blood. On warm spring nights, when the skies are clear and the land is quiet, it's said that Fanny's spirit, eternally hopeful, returns to Dromgoole's Rock to wait again for her lover's return. Many an individual has seen her ghost, an apparition dressed in fashions not seen since the early 19th century, approach the rock and throw herself upon it to weep. It's a pitiful sight, and as the shadows lengthen upon the winding trail that leads to Dromgoole's Rock, it's not hard to imagine, as she once did, that Peter, long and lanky, has returned. Of course, it's only a fool's hope. But who among us hasn't experienced the ache of an unrequited love?

The Phantom Hitchiker

The year was 1924. It was spring, and the night was dark and stormy. A young man—whose name was forgotten long ago, so we will call him Jim—was heading back to his home in High Point after a long night in Raleigh. As he drew near the Highway 70 underpass just outside of Jamestown, the most peculiar sight met his bleary eyes. Standing by the bridge in the pouring rain was a young woman, her white dress clinging gracelessly to her body. She waved frantically at the young man, imploring him to stop. Jim, raised to be a proper Southern gentleman, quickly brought his vehicle to a stop. He threw open his door, rushed to the girl and gallantly draped his coat over her shivering shoulders. For a moment, his breath caught in his throat; he couldn't help but marvel at the girl's beauty. He ushered her toward the passenger seat of his car and within moments they were on their way.

She seemed altogether distracted; she hardly seemed to notice how drenched she was. Water from her tangled, matted dark hair continued to drip down her face like tears. Her gaze was fixed and blank. She rarely blinked; Jim noticed with a shudder how slowly her eyelids closed and opened. When she spoke, it was carefully and deliberately, as if each and every word required close consideration. She asked him to take her to an address in High Point. The young man nodded and then mentioned what a happy coincidence it was that he lived there too.

Concerned, Jim continued to ask her questions. *It's not every day that you see a beautiful young woman stranded by a lonely bridge in the middle of the night*, he thought. But despite his best efforts to learn more about the young woman, her answers proved vague and elusive. All he managed to learn over the next few miles was that her name was Lydia, that she should have been home hours ago and that her mother would be furious. Then she fell silent. The young man's car sped along the slick, gleaming road.

With a sigh of relief, Jim pulled up to the address that Lydia had given him. Smiling, he looked at Lydia, who smiled wanly in return and whispered, "Thank you." He nodded and then turned away from her to get out of the car. In the time it took him to walk around the front of his car to the passenger side to open the door for her, Lydia mysteriously vanished. The young man opened the door and saw nothing but an empty, water-soaked seat. He looked up and down the street but saw no one. He returned to his car and sat with his hands on the steering wheel, wondering what he should do. Remembering how anxious Lydia had seemed to get home to her mother, Jim decided that even though the hour was late, he would at least let Lydia's mother know that he had brought her back, even if she was now nowhere to be found.

Straightening his tie and rearranging his hat, the young man approached the house, walked up to the porch and then hesitantly knocked on the door. There was no response. He knocked again, louder and firmer. A few seconds later, he heard footsteps creaking their way toward the door. The door opened slightly and the face of an older woman poked around the corner. She was undeniably Lydia's mother. Lydia had her eyes.

"What is it?" the older woman snapped. Jim cleared his throat and then began relating the night's events. He'd barely begun when the older woman, her eyes flashing with anger, yelled, "Get out of here! You're a cruel and vicious man." Jim was stung by the words and he stood in a daze on the porch. He began to stammer in protest, unsure exactly what had just happened. He'd only tried to be a Good Samaritan, but there he was, standing soaked on a strange woman's porch, vilified and attacked for his good intentions.

Maybe it was the look of genuine bewilderment in his eyes. Or it could have been something else entirely. But Lydia's mother's demeanor inexplicably transformed. In a hushed, tragic voice, she asked the young man to wait for just a moment. He nodded, determined to see this bizarre and eerie experience through to the end. She padded away and then returned shortly with a photograph in her hand.

She opened the door wide and handed the young man the creased and worn picture. "Is this the girl you saw?" the woman asked in a quivering voice. Jim nodded slowly. "Yes," he answered, "yes it is." The answer sent tears cascading down the woman's cheeks. "That's Lydia," she wept, "my only daughter. She died over a year ago."

Jim was stunned into silence. She ushered him in, and a few minutes later, over a cup of coffee, the young man heard how one evening, Lydia was coming home from a party in Raleigh. She had urged her escort to drive quicker lest she incur her mother's wrath for having missed her curfew. The driver lost control of the car at the Highway 70 underpass, just outside of Jamestown. He was thrown clear of the wreckage but Lydia was killed instantly. Shortly after her daughter was buried, Lydia's mother began receiving visitors, each with eerily similar tales, just like the one Jim had finished recounting. Even in death, it seems, Lydia is determined to make her curfew. Of course, she never does.

To the end of her days, Lydia's mother continued to receive late-night visitors inquiring after the young woman with the raven hair and white dress who had vanished from their cars. Each time, she had to explain all over again what had happened. It seemed as if she was destined to relive the anguish of her daughter's untimely death. When she herself passed away and a new family moved into her house, Lydia continued to appear by the bridge near Jamestown, requesting to be taken back to her home in High Point. The new residents of the house quickly became accustomed to Lydia and made only one request of the young men who appeared on their doorstep: not to reveal the address, lest the information provoke the bored and idle to come around asking all sorts of aggravating questions.

As the years passed, Lydia's legend grew to mythic proportions. It is among the state's most popular and enduring ghost stories. The bridge at which she appears is no longer part of any highway system. It still exists though, draped in a web-like curtain of tangled kudzu vines. By day, the place is desolate and eerie. By night, it becomes a popular destination for the teenagers of nearby Jamestown who gather there to carouse and work on their graffiti skills. The bridge is covered in the stuff, much of it addressed to dearly departed Lydia. She hasn't been seen around the old bridge for quite some time, though some people swear that she's just moved down the road to the newer underpass.

Weeping Arch

Though the summer months are today greeted with joy, it was not always so. For much of American history, summers only heralded the arrival of diseases such as cholera and the dreaded yellow fever. Epidemics were all too common, afflicting both rich and poor, young and old. In 1864, yellow fever swept through Wilmington and in just one month claimed 710 lives, over one-tenth of its population. In time, those who could afford to do so left the fledgling metropolises in the summer to escape the infected masses. Those unable to leave lived out the summer months, dread and anxiety their constant companions.

Doctors of the time had determined that yellow fever was brought to coastal cities by infected seamen returning from the tropics. They didn't suspect that the teeming mosquitoes were most responsible for its spread. Once a mosquito carrying the yellow fever virus bit a healthy individual, the disease began its assault. Within days, the afflicted began complaining of head and body aches, high fever and nausea. As their livers were ravaged, their skin acquired the yellow pallor for which the disease was named. Often, more than half of those afflicted died within days; the ones fortunate enough to survive were blessed with lifelong immunity. To prevent the disease from taking hold, Southern ports created stations of quarantine, demanding that ships returning from abroad anchor for at least a month to guarantee that crews were disease-free. Only then were the ships allowed to dock and unload their cargoes. It wasn't the best system and it often failed to curb yellow fever's spread. Though it was reported as far north as Boston, yellow fever seemed to favor the coastal cities of the South, where the marshes and swamps and pleasant climates proved ideal for mosquitoes to breed.

New Bern was settled in 1710 at the confluence of the Neuse and Trent rivers. It quickly established itself as both a farming and shipping community. Its many plantations produced exports that were shipped all across the world, among them tobacco and cotton. Of course, its prominence as a port contributed directly to the yellow fever epidemic that rampaged through New Bern in 1798.

Within days, people all over New Bern were infected with the disease and the numbers only continued to rise. The first of the dead were buried behind New Bern's Christ Church but its small graveyard soon proved incapable of accommodating the rising number of souls yellow fever had dispatched with frightening efficiency. Trenches were dug within the churchyard, but these too were soon overwhelmed with bodies. Finally, in desperation, church leaders created a cemetery and named it Cedar Grove for the cedar trees that shaded its ground. When the epidemic came to an end in 1799, yellow fever had claimed the lives of 88 people: 47 adults and the rest children. Few of the 500 families in New Bern managed to escape the epidemic untouched. Many families and friends shed tears at Cedar Grove Cemetery and today, the place continues to weep.

With such dark and devastating origins, few people are surprised to hear that Cedar Grove Cemetery is haunted, the home to unexpected and bizarre phenomena. Interred also within its grounds are the fallen Confederates who fought in the Battle of New Bern, as well as more yellow fever victims, many from the epidemic of 1864, which claimed over 300 lives and infected close to 800 people.

In 1854, a great stone triple-arch gateway, carved from marlstone and coquina rock, was erected at Cedar Grove Cemetery. Entry to and exit from Cedar Grove Cemetery is gained only by passing beneath the arch. This arch has puzzled and fascinated people for over a century and a half. Known locally as the Weeping Arch, the gateway is said to rain the blood of the dead upon passing mourners. Most frightening of all is the apocryphal belief that should a drop fall upon your flesh, death will closely follow and you will become a guest of honor at Cedar Grove.

Those with a more rational bent scoff at such claims and point out that the marlstone and coquina rock used in the arch's construction are both porous and therefore collect rainwater that then drips down until the rock has been bled dry. Of course, they're hard pressed to explain how the Weeping Arch continues to weep even when weeks have passed with nary a drop of rain. And then there are the peculiar qualities of the drops themselves. Reddish in color, the drops are plainly visible upon clothing and skin, looking very much like droplets of blood. But maddeningly, they evaporate without a trace. Careful examination of the stone itself has revealed nothing. People who can accept the unexplained simply nod and continue to believe that the Weeping Arch cries for those interred within Cedar Grove Cemetery, for the victims of yellow fever and the Confederate soldiers who died ignobly upon the battlefield. The tears are a grim reminder that death is always close at hand.

The Beautiful Nell Cropsey

In 1898, William Cropsey moved his family from Brooklyn to Elizabeth City in Pasquotank County, North Carolina. They moved into a quaint, gabled riverside home on the aptly named Riverside Avenue. Cropsey had three daughters: Ollie, the older child; Ella Maud, fondly and forever known as Nell, and Gertrude, the youngest. Young and beautiful, with eyes as blue as the ocean and dark, lustrous chestnut hair, Nell caught the eye of many a man, but it was Jim Wilcox, five years her senior and the son of the county sheriff, who caught hers. For three years they dated, but the relationship came to a disturbing and sudden end when, on November 20, 1901, 19-year-old Nell Cropsey disappeared, just days before she was supposed to go back north to visit cousins for Thanksgiving. Her suitor had been the last to see her alive.

Ollie recalled seeing Nell go out on the porch at about 11 PM to talk with Jim. By midnight, Nell still hadn't come in. Ollie assumed that Nell had come in quietly and gone straight to her bedroom, but when she went into her younger sister's room, the bed was undisturbed. As the hours passed, the Cropseys grew more concerned, and finally William decided to go to the Wilcox household. He suspected that Nell and Jim had eloped and that maybe the Wilcox family could provide additional information. He returned later with Jim in tow but the suitor didn't reveal much, insisting that he left a sobbing Nell on the porch. He claimed he'd gone into town and thought Nell had gone back into the house.

Ollie suspected that the evening hadn't been as innocent as Jim claimed. Months before, the two sweethearts had soured on each other and Ollie knew that Nell was no longer interested in pursuing a relationship with the sheriff's son. The day after Nell's disappearance, Jim Wilcox was arrested for kidnapping and suspicion of murder.

When interrogated, he spun a tangled web of stories. He first claimed that he broke off the relationship since she had lately become disinterested, and then later said that she had seemed suicidal and didn't resemble the happy and bright-eyed girl he had fallen in love with. Officials weren't too interested in what he had to say and released him.

A search for Nell began. They searched Riverside Avenue but found nothing there, so they had to widen their focus. Bloodhound expert Hurricane Branch was brought in to join the search, and soon more than 1000 Elizabeth City residents were beating the fields, following the lead of the blood-hounds who had sniffed at Nell's shoes and socks. Citizens noted darkly that Jim Wilcox chose not to participate. Rumors began to swirl: Nell had been kidnapped! She was being held for ransom! She had been thrown into the river! A psychic offered her assistance, claiming that she felt certain that Nell was alive and that she was on a boat. Another clair-voyant, Madame Snell Newman, claimed the opposite. According to Newman, Jim Wilcox had incapacitated the girl with chloroform, wrapped her body in a blanket, taken her to the countryside and murdered her. He had then tossed her lifeless body into a deep well.

The account resonated with Elizabeth City residents. Most of them suspected that Jim Wilcox knew more than he had revealed. He certainly wasn't acting the role of the heartbroken suitor. On December 6, 1901, Madame Snell Newman arrived at the Cropsey house. She sat down in a rocking chair and, looking at the anxious family, said that Jim had sat in the chair. With a tremulous nod, Ollie offered her affirmation. The psychic continued to offer more details, all of them stunningly accurate, and then claimed that Jim had killed Nell in a jealous rage. When he learned that Nell planned on returning to New York for Thanksgiving, he decided that if he couldn't have her, then no one would.

Another search party gathered at the Cropsey house. Following the information provided by Madame Newman, they searched the countryside for miles, walking down one fruitless trail after another. They did stumble across two wells but neither contained a body. It didn't really matter. Madame Newman's scandalous premonitions had all but indicted Jim Wilcox in the minds of Elizabeth City. It didn't seem to matter much that the psychic had been wildly off the mark on a number of her claims. Indeed, the most glaring and obvious error was that for all the psychic's predictions, Nell's body had yet to be found. In yet another twist, in December, an anonymous letter was received. Contained within it was a simple map, with an X marking the alleged location of Nell's body. Surprisingly, authorities gave the letter scant attention.

Five days later, on December 27, 1901, two men fishing in the Pasquotank River made a gruesome discovery not far from the location marked on the mysterious map. What they initially assumed to be a log actually turned out to be the floating bloated corpse of Nell Cropsey. Her autopsy was inconclusive, though the coroner was able to determine that Nell had not drowned. He pointed to a suspicious bruise on her forehead as a sign of murder. When word of the discovery and the autopsy reached Elizabeth City residents, they formed a mob. Thirsty for retribution, they demanded the immediate lynching of Jim Wilcox. Jim, who continued to profess his innocence, was jailed while the mob frothed and foamed outside his cell. It took a desperate plea from William Cropsey to finally disperse the bloodthirsty crowd.

In 1902, Jim was convicted of first-degree murder and sentenced to death by hanging. Despite the nagging lack of any physical evidence tying him to Nell's death, strong public sentiment, bolstered by the claims of Madame Snell Newman, carried the day. Cooler heads eventually prevailed and the state Supreme Court declared a mistrial. Jim was tried again, this time in Perquimans County. In his second trial, he was convicted of second-degree murder and sentenced to 30 years in prison.

With the matter seemingly settled, the Cropseys departed Elizabeth City, tired of the national publicity Nell's death had generated. Ollie retreated into seclusion. As the years passed, it seemed as if Nell's murder had set in motion a bizarre series of events. In 1908, Roy Crawford, who had called on Ollie the night Nell disappeared, shot himself. Five years later, William Cropsey Jr., Nell's younger brother, poisoned himself in Norfolk, Virginia.

Jim Wilcox was pardoned for his crime in 1918 by Governor Thomas Walter Bickett. On Christmas Eve, Jim Wilcox returned to Elizabeth City. He would have done just as well to remain in prison. Tainted forever by his alleged involvement in Nell's death, he became a pariah. Unable to find work, Jim grew despondent and turned increasingly to the bottle to alleviate his pain. In 1932, he and W.O. Saunders, editor of the local newspaper, *The Independent*, began plans to collaborate on a book about the Nell Cropsey case. Two years later, Jim summoned the editor to his room to talk. Just two weeks after, Jim Wilcox put a shotgun against his skull and blew off his head

What had he told the editor? Had he finally revealed what had happened to Nell Cropsey? Nobody would ever know. The editor died shortly after in an accident; whatever passed between him and Wilcox has never been disclosed. To this day, no one knows for certain what happened that November night, and the strange events that followed have only shrouded the case in mystery and doubt.

It's a tragedy that refuses to rest. Few Elizabeth City residents nowadays do not know the enigma that is Nell Cropsey. Not only does she lurk within the town's consciousness, she continues to call the house at 1901 Riverside Avenue home. If only her spirit could speak…perhaps then the age-old mystery of her death could be put to rest. Until then, she continues to roam the halls of Cropsey House, a beloved houseguest of those who live with her.

Today, the Caruso family lives in the house formerly occupied by the Cropsey family, and they have fully embraced their ghostly houseguest. Though previous tenants have claimed that Nell's specter has been an unwelcome presence in their daily lives, Robin Caruso believes exactly the opposite. In an interview with Jeffery Hampton of *The Virginian Pilot*, Robin Caruso stated confidently that she believes it's her family's destiny to live in the Cropsey house and because of that, Nell proves more than accommodating. "We're supposed to be here," she said and proceeded to describe her family's connection with the Cropseys.

Robin's husband Frank grew up in New York and remembers buying vegetables from the Cropsey Farm. The Elizabeth City Cropseys were part of that same family of Cropseys. Frank's father had been a banker and had helped secure the financing for the Cropsey Farm subdivision that was developed on Cropsey land. Frank and Robin had lived in Elizabeth City before and had long wanted to own the historic home.

Robin tells of Nell appearing unexpectedly in bedrooms, and she describes the mournful and melancholy visage of Nell's mother appearing in the house's windows, ever hopeful that her daughter will soon return. These accounts are fascinating and, unlike many haunted homeowners, the Carusos have embraced the spirits. They've even allowed groups of curious people to walk through the home and will lovingly point out a name etched into the wall lining the staircase. The inscription bears the name of Gertrude, one of Nell's sisters, and is dated 1903, not long before the Cropseys left the area.

Of course, not all of the Carusos are delighted with the spirits. In the late 90s, Ryan Caruso was 14 and was walking down the hall near his bedroom when he saw something that literally took his breath away. Standing just outside his room was a woman, her long, dark chestnut hair tied loosely at the nape of her neck, long, curly tresses framing her face. Her smooth skin was the color of alabaster, and her eyes were a shade of blue so deep and rich they almost seemed unnatural. She wore a prim Victorian dress, its collar fastened closely around her neck. She peered at Ryan for a moment and then, as if losing interest, turned around. The specter so frightened the child that he tried to scream but unable to form any sound. He just stood there and gasped until finally his voice returned and he began calling out for his parents. When they heard him, they rushed to his side but Nell had vanished into the ether from which she had appeared.

In 2001, in an effort to attract attention to Elizabeth City's history, the first annual Elizabeth City Ghost Walk took place. Among its many stops, which included seven historic homes, two churches, a cemetery and a century-old community building, was the Cropsey house. Recruited to play Nell Cropsey and to impart some authenticity and immediacy to the walk was a local girl, Christy Beacham, whose birthday is November 20, the day on which Nell disappeared so many years ago. At the time, chairwoman Patsy Houtz had slim expectations of the event. "I expect we'll do this every year if it's halfway successful," she said to *The Virginian Pilot*. It was a success, and the Elizabeth City Ghost Walk has become an annual, highly anticipated event.

As for Nell Cropsey and her still-unsolved murder, locals have their theories. Robin Caruso believes that her death was a collaboration between Jim Wilcox and, shockingly, Nell's father. Whatever anyone might think, Nell Cropsey's death will most likely never be solved but the continued presence of her restless spirit pretty much guarantees that no one will ever stop trying. It's the most anyone can do for the beautiful girl whose life came to such an abrupt and ignoble end.

Theodosia Burr

In late December 1812, a ship named the *Patriot* sat waiting in the harbor of Georgetown (now Charleston), South Carolina. Despite reports of British warships patrolling the Atlantic coasts, the threat of rampant piracy and an expected storm, the *Patriot* set sail. Aboard the ship was the auburn-haired, beautiful and sickly Theodosia Burr, daughter of erstwhile U.S. vice-president Aaron Burr, on her way to visit her famous father in New York. Her husband, South Carolina Governor Joseph Alston, waved farewell, but he was unaware that the *Patriot* sailed not for the ports of New York but into oblivion. Theodosia Burr would never be seen alive again. Her spirit, on the other hand, is believed to roam the waters of Cape Hatteras, North Carolina.

The *Patriot* failed to arrive at its scheduled time in New York. A desperate Aaron Burr feared the worst and an intensive search and rescue operation, sailing as far south as Nassau, combed the Atlantic coast to find the missing ship. Though she had sailed along a well-traveled sea-lane, no merchant ships could recall encountering the *Patriot*. Accusers pointed their fingers at Great Britain, alleging that its warships must have sunk the *Patriot*. London insisted that it had nothing to do with the ship's disappearance, and Alston himself believed the theory to be untrue. He had written a letter, stating that his wife was on board and guaranteeing the ship safe passage. Others claimed that pirates must have boarded the ship, while still others believed that it had been destroyed in a hurricane. It mattered little. The ship had vanished.

Theodosia Burr, despite her privileged upbringing, had lived a life of tragedy. Her mother had passed away in 1794 and left her father to raise her. He did so ably, and Theodosia grew into a well-read, educated and refined young woman whose auburn hair flamed as brightly as her temperament. As a 16-year-old, Theodosia could converse with ease in six different languages and spoke knowledgeably on subjects like economics and politics. She was a charming figure, and among those who fell under her spell was Joseph Alston. On a visit to New York, he met and quickly became enamored with Theodosia, to Aaron Burr's great consternation. Burr felt Alston was a poor match for his daughter, inapt for a woman of such standing. After all, Burr was one of the leading lights of the United States. He had fought alongside George Washington during the American Revolution and had lost a closely contested election for the presidency to Thomas Jefferson. He served, instead, as Jefferson's vice-president. Not just anyone, and certainly not Alston, could marry his daughter.

Alston was determined to win Burr's favor. As soon as he returned to South Carolina, he sent Burr missive after missive, each proclaiming not only his ardor for Theodosia, but also his social standing. He reminded Burr that while he may have inherited The Oaks plantation from his grandfather, he had become a success in his own right. He attended Princeton and became a lawyer before he was 20 and his ambitions included the state's governorship. With his wealth and resources, he assured Burr that Theodosia would not want for anything. Burr, still somewhat reluctant, finally assented to the union and Theodosia and Joseph were married in February 1801 in Albany, New York. The newly minted couple decamped to South Carolina.

Life in the South disagreed with Theodosia. She found The Oaks nothing but an "island of swamp lands" and sorely missed the cosmopolitan refinery of metropolitan New York City, where men and women led intellectual lives. As she looked at the women around her, she found their frilly dresses and their insatiable thirst for gossip numbing. It was all a waste. Theodosia took to spending more and more time in her bed. The humidity and mosquitoes of the South ravaged Theodosia's health and she became increasingly frail, finding relief only in the visage of her newborn son, Aaron Burr Alston. When her father's political feud with Alexander Hamilton (whom he blamed for his loss of the presidency) climaxed in the famous Burr-Hamilton duel of 1804, Burr found himself a pariah thanks to Hamilton's powerful friends, who exacted revenge for Hamilton's death. Theodosia grew ever more convinced that moving to South Carolina had been a grievous mistake. Alston, for his part, did what he could to comfort Theodosia but was largely absent as he attended to his political career in Charleston.

Constantly ill, Theodosia resolved to move from the plantation to a summer cottage on the coast. The climate did restore some of Theodosia's health but she and Alston paid a heavy price for it. Their young son fell ill with a head cold and despite the frantic work of several physicians, his malarial fever could not be cured. He died, and Theodosia wrote to her father, "My dear father… there is no more joy for me, the world is a blank. I have lost my boy. My child is gone forever."

Burr had recently returned to New York after a fruitless and embarrassing trip to Europe to restore his depleted fortune and political credibility. His career, once ascendant, was now tarnished by his involvement in a treasonous plot to create a new republic from the states west of the Appalachians to Mexico. Burr was frantic to see his sickly daughter and insisted she come to New York to visit. Theodosia agreed and journeyed to Charleston with her husband, to set sail for New York in December 1812.

Weeks after the *Patriot* went missing off the North Carolina coast, the citizens of Nags Head, North Carolina, woke to a most disturbing and shocking sight. Beached on the shore was a schooner that bore more than a passing resemblance to the *Patriot*. It could have been the ship but it was impossible to tell for certain because it had been stripped of all identifying marks. No crew was left aboard to answer the many questions the curious had, and the only living thing aboard was an emaciated black kitten mewling in the pantry. In one cabin, investigators found a number of fancy silk dresses and a vase from which spilled a bouquet of flowers. Could it have been Theodosia's cabin?

Years passed. Joseph Alston passed away in 1816, and Aaron Burr in 1836, neither of them ever discovering the true nature of Theodosia's fate. No one else had either. Then, in 1869, an Elizabeth City doctor was called out to a Nags Head fisherman's house to treat a most peculiar patient. As the fisherman and his wife looked on anxiously, he began his examination of a wizened old woman. The woman seemed confused, and the doctor learned from the couple that they had encountered the strange woman years ago, wandering the Outer Banks. She bore one possession: a portrait of herself. Her sanity and memories appeared to have been borne out with the tide. The doctor did what he could, but he quietly assured the couple that death was now inevitable.

He approached the couple and asked for his fee. They asked him if he would instead accept something from their house, as they had no money. The doctor thought about it for a moment and then inclined his head. He pointed to an elegant portrait hanging on the wall. The aged woman, suddenly lucid, leapt from her bed with a surprising agility and threw herself in front of the portrait. "It's mine," she yelled. "You will not take it! I'm on my way to visit my father in New York and he will have this picture of his darling Theodosia!" She grabbed the portrait and hurried through the door and out into the Atlantic. She was never seen again. The portrait washed ashore the following morning.

The good doctor, who had remained in Nags Head for the evening lest the strange woman should return, took possession of the portrait with a curious look. It was obviously a rendering of the old woman in younger days and her face was familiar to him. She bore more than a passing resemblance to Theodosia Burr, the woman who had vanished without a trace so many years ago. With the portrait in hand, he returned to Elizabeth City and compared it to other portraits. He then knew for sure that the woman had been none other than Theodosia Burr. With her last words, she had most likely re-enacted her last terrifying moments aboard the *Patriot,* which, it was now patently clear, must have been boarded by pirates.

No one will ever know for certain what happened to Theodosia Burr. There are other accounts stating that she ended up in Texas and that she died in the arms of a Karankawa Indian chief. The intervening years have only clouded the mystery though there are few along North Carolina's Outer Banks who deny that Theodosia Burr continues to roam its shores.

Many visitors to North Carolina's Huntington Beach State Park, seeking nothing more than the sand, sun and surf, have come away a little rattled. They've often watched with a mix of curiosity and fear as a woman garbed in a Victorian dress walks across the sand toward the surf and into the ocean. People call out to her, but she seems not to hear their warnings and continues along her way. Most eerily of all, when she reaches the foaming waters of the Atlantic, she sinks not into the surf but hovers above it, until finally her figure is lost in the mist. It must surely be Theodosia Burr, tracing her last steps on earth, determined still to reach her father.

Roan Mountain

Though Roan Mountain, at 6285 feet, is not technically a mountain (it's really a high ridge spanning five miles), it towers above the imagination. For centuries, people have found its peak fascinating, and have been drawn to the location not just by its plentiful flora but also by the stories that cascaded down from its slopes. It is home not just to a singularly spectacular phenomenon known as the circular rainbow, but also to what the earliest settlers called the angelic choir.

Cherokee tribes once roamed Roan Mountain and the surrounding lands, but they receded into history with the arrival of European settlers who found Roan Mountain particularly unique. Botanists flocked to its fields to study its plant life. Among them were the famed Andre Michaux, Dr. Asa Gray (reputed father of American botany and discoverer of a new species of red-orange lily upon Roan Mountain) and John Fraser, the man who discovered a spectacular "new plant" on his travels: rhododendron catawbiense. Every summer, over 600 acres of these rhododendrons bloom, creating an explosion of red, pink and all shades of lavender, visible as far away as Bakersville, 12 miles off. It is known today as the world's largest natural garden of its sort. Explorers marveled at its crest and its balds, the treeless, lush grassy areas that cover Roan Mountain.

Majestic fir and spruce are found here too, and they combine to form an ecosystem that is plentiful in the northern climes of Canada but rare in the Southern U.S. Early settlers quickly baptized the ridge The Roan. Some believe it to be a reference to the spectacular rhododendron blooms, while

Roan Mountain is home to a circular rainbow and an angelic choir.

others claim that the name traces back to Daniel Boone. According to legend, Boone left his roan horse on the balds and continued west. When he returned, he discovered that his steed had grown fat and supple on the rich grasses of the balds. The Roan is a fascinating place, a site that in the 1830s Dr. Elisha Mitchell, a University of North Carolina professor for whom Mitchell County was named, called "the most beautiful of all the high mountains. The top of the Roan…is a vast meadow without a tree to obstruct this prospect…A green ocean of mountains rising in tremendous billows."

Near its peak, the withered and timbered remains of the once-regal 166-room Cloudland Hotel hints at The Roan's past. Erected in 1885, it was the temporary home of amateur botanists who, in addition to exploring the flora and the vista, were treated to the spectacular sight of a circular rainbow: a divine ring of color suspended in the sky as if hung there by the hand of God Himself. Few of the botanists had ever seen such a thing and they often watched the skies eagerly after rains fell on the North Carolina side of the mountain (the Roan straddles the border between North Carolina and Tennessee) and the sun in the western sky bathed the mountaintop with their light.

Since the mountain is devoid of the muggy heat and incessant mosquitoes of the lowlands, early settlers thought that The Roan, with its unobstructed vistas, waterfalls and springs of sweet water and its thornless blackberry bushes, was a special place. A distinct, unearthly music swept down the slopes, bathing its unsuspecting audience in a chorus that could only be attributed to the divine.

The earliest settlers described the music as a "choir of angels" and so too did Cloudland hotelier John Thomas Wilder, who had heard it himself long ago and then passed the story along to interested guests at the hotel. According to Nancy Roberts and her collection of ghost stories, *North Carolina Ghosts and Legends*, a young scientist from Knoxville, Tennessee named Henry Colton described it as follows: "Several of the cattle tenders on the mountain and also Colonel Wilder had spoken to us about [the] 'Mountain Music.' One evening they said it was sounding loud…The sound was very plain to the ear. It was always loudest and most prolonged just after a thunderstorm…I used every argument I could to persuade myself that it simply was a result of some common cause."

He later theorized that the sound must have been caused by air currents meeting each other in the valley between two peaks of The Roan. But for those who had heard it, such an explanation seemed too pedestrian and too banal for so sublime and sweet a sound. Colton may have remained a skeptic, but for most, experiencing the unearthly music of Roan Mountain is akin to communing with the divine.

The music starts low, almost inaudible but undeniable. As the cloudy skies from a passing thunderstorm part and the sun appears from behind its veil, the chorus intensifies, sounding less like the howling wind, which many initially presume it to be, and more like a choir of hundreds of voices singing together in perfect harmony in a wave of sweetness that washes over the balds. It builds and builds, rising to a crashing crescendo that moves from forte to mezzo forte and then finally, to a rousing fortissimo. Then it dies, and silence takes its place. To hear the chorus is to know perfection; here, surely, is the voice of heaven itself. As the wind blows across the balds, many turn their gaze to the skies where the great circular rainbow now hangs. "God's halo," the people call it, and it's the only fitting conclusion to one of North Carolina's greatest phenomena.

The End

GHOST HOUSE BOOKS

Add To Your Ghost House Collection With These New Titles Full of Fascinating Mysteries and Terrifying Tales.

Scary Stories
by Andrew Warwick

A fun collection of creepy tales, from twisted urban legends and laugh-out-loud absurdities to paranormal phenomena. Three men stranded by a scheming tour guide find out why their destination is called "Cannibal Falls." Having died of shame thanks to a bell tied around its neck, a cat's bitter spirit seeks revenge on its owner. A selfish American business-man acquires a mummy with a haunted past—and pays the price for his greed. And much more!

$10.95USD/$14.95CDN • ISBN 1-894877-61-6 • 5.25" x 8.25" • 224 pages

Premonitions and Psychic Warnings
by Edrick Thay

Since the dawn of time, people have experienced premonitions. Some foretell disasters, while others help to prevent them. A soldier who can smell emotions and see death helps his troop avoid a military ambush in the jungle. On a prairie highway, a woman encounters an eyeless hitchhiker who bears more than a passing resemblance to her ailing aunt. A vision of twisted metal and broken glass saves a reckless girl from a car accident. These are just some of the eyewitness accounts explored by author Edrick Thay as he studies the remarkable effects of superhuman perception on the lives of ordinary people.

$10.95USD/$14.95CDN • ISBN 1-894877-58-6 • 5.25" x 8.25" • 232 pages

Famous People of the Paranormal
by Chris Wangler

Shamans, psychics, yogis, channelers—almost every culture singles out people with extraor-dinary gifts. This ambitious book explores the bizarre lives of paranormal celebrities through the ages. As you might imagine, not everyone in this unusual field is genuine; author Chris Wangler also exposes a handful of bona fide paranormal charlatans.

$10.95USD/$14.95CDN • ISBN 1-894877-45-4 • 5.25" x 8.25" • 240 pages

These and many more Ghost House books are available from your local bookseller or by ordering direct. U.S. readers call 1-800-518-3541. In Canada, call 1-800-661-9017.